Love or die trying

**BOB
RAMSAY**

HOW
I LOST IT ALL,
DIED, AND
CAME BACK
FOR LOVE

Love
or die
trying

DUNDURN
PRESS

Publisher: Scott Fraser | Editor: Russell Smith
Cover design: Paul Haslip, HM&E Design Communications
Cover image: Bill Allen, Unsplash
Printer: Marquis Book Printing Inc.
Text in chapters 16 and 17 first appeared in "Life After Near Death: 'I Marvel at My Heart and the New Life It's Given Me.'" *Maclean's*, September 24, 2012. macleans.ca/society/health/a-ticking-time-bomb/. Used with permission.

Library and Archives Canada Cataloguing in Publication

Title: Love or die trying : how I lost it all, died, and came back for love / Bob Ramsay.
Names: Ramsay, Bob, 1949- author.
Identifiers: Canadiana (print) 20210121874 | Canadiana (ebook) 20210121939 | ISBN 9781459747173 (softcover) | ISBN 9781459747180 (PDF) | ISBN 9781459747197 (EPUB)
Subjects: LCSH: Ramsay, Bob, 1949-—Family. | LCSH: Marmoreo, Jean—Family. | LCGFT: Autobiographies.
Classification: LCC CT310.R36 A3 2021 | DDC 971.07092—dc23

We acknowledge the support of the Canada Council for the Arts and the Ontario Arts Council for our publishing program. We also acknowledge the financial support of the Government of Ontario, through the Ontario Book Publishing Tax Credit and Ontario Creates, and the Government of Canada.

Care has been taken to trace the ownership of copyright material used in this book. The author and the publisher welcome any information enabling them to rectify any references or credits in subsequent editions.

The publisher is not responsible for websites or their content unless they are owned by the publisher.

Printed and bound in Canada.

Dundurn Press
1382 Queen Street East
Toronto, Ontario, Canada M4L 1C9
dundurn.com, @dundurnpress 🐦 f 📷

For Jean

*It's too bad
we screwed up
our friendship*

We all have our broken pieces.... In this life, nobody gets away unhurt. We're always trying to find somebody whose broken pieces fit with our broken pieces, and something whole emerges.

— Bruce Springsteen

PROLOGUE The End of the Beginning

It's said that 90 percent of interventions led by friends or family members fail, while 90 percent of those led by a professional interventionist succeed. By *succeed*, I don't mean that the person being intervened on stops drinking or doing drugs for the rest of their lives; I mean they take the first step to getting help to stop. This usually means attending meetings of Alcoholics Anonymous or its many variants, or agreeing to go to treatment in a rehabilitation facility.

In my case, there was no time to find a professional, and I was too far down the hole of my addiction to give stopping more than a frantic passing thought.

My best friend Charles Fremes was worried about me. A month earlier, I'd had to borrow money from him to take a train home after a wedding in Montreal.

My accountant, Arthur Gelgoot, had warned me, "Just don't get arrested." My denial was so tight that I was offended by Arthur's words. How did he know? How dare he think I'd run afoul of the law?

Of course, as with most alcoholics and addicts, everyone knew. Why did my staff of ten all drift into jobs elsewhere? They knew. Why was I huddling in a tiny office that I'd bargained for with my landlord after giving up our entire floor upstairs? She knew. Why were the tenants in my triplex dropping their cheques in my mailbox and not ringing the doorbell to chat? They knew. As for the police, it's a miracle they didn't pull me over as I inched my way home in my car, terrified of exceeding the thirty kilometre per hour speed limit, and instead driving only twenty.

Addiction is a way to push people away.

But Charles and Arthur hung in there. Once, many months after they engineered my intervention, Charles said to me, "You grossly underestimate the depth of our friendship if you think you can run away from me — and us."

Charles and Arthur were also well aware that I'd never sit still for an intervention. So, Charles called me one night. "Arthur and I want to meet with you to do some long-term business planning. How about tomorrow afternoon?"

I was flattered. Long-range business planning implied a number of things that were no longer true: that I had a business, that I was able to plan anything beyond my next high, and that my long-range future looked even possible.

At some level, I knew this was the intervention that I'd both dreaded and desperately hoped for. That's the thing about addiction: a rare glimpse of reality will occasionally seep through the tightly held denial. It's in those brief moments that change can happen.

All the next morning, I was tempted to call my friends and cancel. But I was just so tired and lonely, and so hurt that my willpower could do nothing to help me stop. So, I waited for the knock on my office door at 2:00 p.m. The door was locked, of course, because that's what addicts do.

When they arrived, Charles kept the mood light, just like old times, with lots of witty chit-chat. Then he pulled out a piece of paper. "Arthur and I have done up an agenda for our meeting so we can use our time efficiently."

Again, I was flattered. This sounded like I just had to do a little planning and everything would soon be shipshape.

He handed me the paper. There were half a dozen items on it — "Clients," "Staffing," "Taxes" — but item number one was "Improving Your Health."

"So we need to talk about your health first," Arthur began, "because if you're not prepared to work on that, then there's really nothing to say about the other items."

"My health?" I asked.

They were tired of my denial. "Your *cocaine addiction*."

"Right. Yes, of course."

"You need to give yourself a break. We think you need to go away to get better … We've found a place for you —"

"Really?" I was so grateful I almost broke down in tears. This hell would soon end. I could start over. They cared! Charles and Arthur were the cavalry, and the cavalry had finally come to rescue me.

"It's a treatment centre outside Atlanta."

"Atlanta? Why so far away? I can't go there. I've got things to do here." My denial was preventing me from grasping the lifeline they had thrown me.

"Like what?" asked Charles.

"Well … like …" Actually, there wasn't a single thing I could think of that was holding me back from seeking treatment. I had no kids, no work, no relationship, and I was fast pushing away my few remaining friends.

Arthur stepped in. "Don't worry, we'll pay the bills when you're gone."

But I was terrified that people would find out, and worse, talk.

Again, as I would learn when I intervened on dozens of others in the thirty years since then, we addicts have a huge fear, not just that someone will learn our secret, but that they'll tell others about it.

Somehow, Charles and Arthur, who'd never intervened on anyone in their lives, got this part right, too.

"You can just tell people you're taking a creative break in Banff, maybe doing some courses at the Banff School."

That was perfect. I'm from Alberta, and had taken summer courses in Banff when I was a teen. So, I had a cover story.

"What's the treatment centre?" I asked.

"It's called Talbott Recovery Center. We've checked it out for you and they have a space open. They can take you tomorrow. I'll fly down with you. There's an 8:00 a.m. flight."

Whoa … whoa … The twin panics of getting well and being deprived of my drug took over.

"Tomorrow?"

"Sure, why not?"

"Because I've got lots to do!"

"Like what?"

"Like …"

Of course I had nothing to do.

"You have a passport?"

"Yes."

"Good," said Arthur. "I'll pick you up at five thirty tomorrow morning at your house. Meanwhile, you'll need to call the people at Talbott. We talked to them yesterday, but they need to hear from you directly that you want to come. They won't take you unless *you* call them."

They made it sound like a marvellous adventure, which is another reason I said the words every interventionist prays for: "Yes, I'll go."

I was so incredibly relieved the pain would soon end that I forgot to push them about why Atlanta instead of someplace in Toronto. I later learned that I was headed to Talbott because, earlier that week, Charles had called his father, a doctor who vaguely knew me through his son, and asked him which was the best treatment centre for me in Toronto.

What Dr. Fremes said next may well have saved my life: "You don't want to send him to Bellwood or Homewood or Donwood. He'll just charm his way through them and come out thirty days later just as addicted. From what you say, Bob Ramsay needs long-term treatment. You should send him to where we send the doctors."

The entire intervention took no longer than fifteen minutes, and as he walked out the door, Arthur pointed his finger at me. "Call them."

I did call, but it took me a few hours to build up my courage — and I was stoned when I dialed the phone. The very minute my friends left, I wrote a company cheque to "Cash," signed it, and took it to my cocaine dealer, who gave me three grams of coke. I wasn't sure I had the money to cover that $450, but I knew that banks didn't bounce cheques made out to Cash.

Ah, the cunning of the not so innocent.

And the iron grip of addiction.

INTRODUCTION Dying for Love

This book was originally going to be a death story.

It would open after I almost died following open-heart surgery in 2011, and close on my speculations surrounding my second death, which would take place in the arms of my wife, Jean Marmoreo, who happens to be an assisted-death doctor. These co-incidences would form the perfect anchors to a memoir filled with other near-death and near-love experiences.

Then my friend and agent, Michael Levine, said something that changed everything: "Bob, anyone who knows you for more than thirty seconds knows the defining thing in your life isn't your death; it's your wife. Don't write your death story. Write your love story."

I was thrilled at the prospect of doing this — but also fearful. Thrilled because, of course, Michael was right: by all odds, given our pasts and our personalities, Jean and I should be the least likely to have built a life together, let alone one filled with such comfort and joy. Thrilled also because a happy, adventurous marriage needs all the celebration it can muster. But afraid, because writing about your own love and marriage is never easy. Though I am a very public and gregarious person, Jean is very private. And as in any marriage, there are always things best left unspoken, and not necessarily the bad things. Despite the fact that both Jean and I write and speak in public, often about deeply personal things like addiction and failure and death, we're not the kind of people who talk much about our relationship and the love that's made so much possible.

In fact, we hardly ever talk about our relationship — at least, not with each other. We're too busy working and taking on life.

For Jean, who is well known as a Boston Marathon runner, a family doctor, a writer and adventurer, I think this impulse comes from growing up with three sisters on a southern Ontario farm in the 1940s. Her dad was old school, tough, and very clear on what was right and wrong. Her mom was a homemaker.

Doing chores on the farm was like breathing. You did them because you always did. You never questioned it. You knew that the punishment for not doing chores would be swift and sure. Better to keep breathing. By the time Jean got to high school, she had learned that hard work could take her further.

No one in the family had gone beyond high school or thought it would be of any benefit. But Jean bridled against her father's strict rule. Her defiance pushed her forward. In 1960, she got into the nursing program at McMaster University in Hamilton, and within a week of graduating was on the bus to Toronto, where she got a job at the Lakeshore Psychiatric Centre. Two years later, she was the head nurse at the then Clarke Institute, which is now CAMH, the Centre for Addiction and Mental Health.

While it was a heady experience being the head nurse, Jean quickly saw that no matter how high you rose as a nurse, the only people with real authority were the doctors. So she decided to apply to medical school. Today, well over 60 percent of medical students in Canada are women. It was nowhere near that in 1971 when Jean applied to the University of Toronto School of Medicine, which was then, and still is, the largest medical school in North America.

She somehow got an appointment with the dean and made her case as a mature student. Back then, being a nurse wasn't seen as an advantage in getting into medical school: it was a drawback.

But not as bad as being married, which Jean was the year before, to Toronto ad executive Rene Marmoreo. And certainly not as bad as being pregnant, which Jean also was.

The dean was not impressed. He said if Jean did well in makeup summer courses in organic chemistry, he wouldn't support her, but he wouldn't blackball her, either.

She worked hard, did well, and got in; the oldest person by far in her class.

In a second-year cardiac tutorial, which was held in one of the med school's labs, Jean put her six-week-old daughter in one of the lab sinks, to sleep during the class. She was in the middle of learning how to read an electrocardiogram when the instructor looked up and yelled, "My god, there's a baby in the sink!"

"Yes, she's mine," said Jean and then carried on.

Leaving your baby to sleep in the lab sink didn't happen much those days; nor did leaving your Saturday morning rounds as an intern: Jean, having been on call all night, had to get home to her baby.

But it was here that she had a graduate education in making your own way in the world.

One of her lab mates was Carolyn Bennett, who happened to be the youngest person in the class. But it wasn't until they were both assigned to internships at Wellesley Hospital to deliver babies that they actually met. In the middle of an interminable lecture on how to be an intern, Jean turned to Carolyn and said, "I think we need a drink." And so was born a close friendship that has lasted to this day.

Years later, Carolyn led many fights for Women's College Hospital's independence, eventually leaving medicine altogether to take up politics full-time. In 1997 she became the member of parliament for Toronto–St. Paul's, a riding she's held now for twenty-four years. She is the current minister of Crown-Indigenous Relations.

Meanwhile, Jean was busy practising family medicine and raising a family that would eventually have three kids. Life was busy, if not especially happy.

Jean would tell me stories of "hiding out in the delivery suite" — using her busyness delivering babies to hide the cracks in her marriage. It was the perfect cover. What could possibly be more important, or angelic, than bringing new life into the world?

But what did work for Jean was hard work. She grew up with it. Got ahead with it. Was rewarded for it, and used it to hide her unhappiness.

Her enormous capacity for work, coupled with a remarkable ability to focus, and my relentless cheering on, have transformed her over the years from an around-the-block runner to a Boston Marathon champion, from a basement woodworker into a master woodworker, from a weekend hiker into a world explorer, and from a woman with lots to say into a columnist for the *Globe and Mail* and the *National Post*, and the author of two books.

As for me, I once told an English professor I had worked very hard on a term paper. She replied, "Bob, I'm not sure you worked hard. I know you worked with a lot of energy." As with so many signals I received in early adulthood, I failed to see the difference.

After graduating from Princeton University in the U.S., I came back to Canada and settled in Toronto. I knew how to write. Just as important, I was confident I knew how to write. My first job was as a speech writer in the office of Premier William Davis. A year later, I became a copywriter at a big ad agency; and two years after that, I became a book editor. Then back to the Premier's Office for another year.

It was all very heady — and forgiving. When you're in your twenties, it's fine to jump from job to job after each year or so. But not in your thirties. So I simply incorporated my inability to hold a job for long and started and built (and brought down) two communications companies over the next decade. For the past thirty years, I've basically headed a virtual company of two full-time employees, plus a tiger of a part-time business manager, who brings on people as needed to help with our speaker series, RamsayTalks, which hosts some of the world's leading authors, like Niall Ferguson, Susan Rice, Garry Kasparov, and John Grisham; our travel company, Ramsay Travels, which promises "group travel for people who don't do group travel"; plus our two writing-related companies, Ramsay Writes, where I write speeches and communications materials for senior executives, and Ramsay Trains, where I teach corporate executives how to stop speaking and writing corporatese.

All of which is to say I started as a writer and will end as a writer.

Lots of people do a lot and talk a lot. Jean does a lot and only talks when pushed to. I do a lot and talk and talk and talk ... but never about why, or how I feel about it. The idea of *doing* as a substitute for *feeling* is something we both learned as young kids.

While our childhoods were very different, they both had a lot of silence. Mine more so, because I grew up without brothers and sisters.

For Jean and me, I suspect so much went unspoken that we had to learn from watching and from the holes between the silences.

But that was all back then, well over half a century ago.

This is now.

If anything these days, we grab life by the neck and throttle it. This scares some people. They ask, "What's your plan for the years ahead?" By this they mean "*When are you going to retire?*" Our answer is always this: "Retire? Why would we ever retire from the work we do now?" Others mean *"How can you possibly keep up this pace?"* What I tell them is that we're going to live our lives at the pace we do — until we can't.

I'm seventy-two and Jean's seventy-nine. We are officially old. Okay, very old. But our lives are so busy, our energy so high, and our work so intense and meaningful, why would we give all this up to ... to do what, exactly?

Jean spends her days listening to people describe their physical and psychological ills. She's a professional listener who tries to dig out what's really going on behind years of silence, deflection, and avoidance. She knows that retirement can be a death sentence for some people. Besides, when you live life this fast and full, it's hard to stop. It's a drug.

I learned this the hard way in March of 2020, the Year of the Plague. In one week, I lost nearly all my work and income. Jean was busy doing telemedicine, either from our apartment in downtown Toronto or from our cottage up north, where we fled to manage some "social distancing." But I had to adjust to no personal contact with people, when I had built my life and work on personal contact. Extroverts don't do well in plagues.

Of course age will slow us down, but to us age and slowing down are open to interpretation. Given where and how we travel, the odds of our falling off a mountain are actually pretty good. And, realistically, disease and death are never far away. As Jean has said, if the mountain scenario fails to materialize, "you're going to stroke out and I'll get hit by a car."

My sweet. My darling. Thank you for that, for softening the blow.

But the fact is that Jean has been a family physician for more than forty-five years. She knows the patterns and the odds.

With her, there's no sugar-coating what lies ahead. Better to deal with it straight up. Or at least talk about it under a cover of frankness.

Like most couples, we have our unspoken idiosyncrasies and habits that signal everything's okay, or not. Over time, they have become a private language between us. No one else has ever spoken this exact dialect before, and no one ever will again. A raised eyebrow speaks volumes, telling me: "Don't push that argument. I'll push back." A sparkling eye (how *do* you make an eye sparkle?) tells me: "Keep going!"

There are billions of couples alive today. Every single couple of us creates our own secret code. I think ours happens to be rich simply because we were raised as kids in a world of codes where keeping one wasn't a choice, but an imperative.

Not every couple wants to write a book about their relationship. In fact, hardly anyone does. Note that Jean is not my co-author here.

But I believe our strange and ongoing story is worth telling because it can give hope to others who feel that life hasn't really started yet for them, especially those in midlife. Or who feel that life is not worth living. Or that some fatal personal flaw keeps them from anything more than muddling through. Because I felt all of those things, sometimes for many years. All it took was the extraordinary luck of meeting and falling for a woman who was not my type at all and who intimidated the hell out of me.

If you're at the start of your adult life, this story can act as a cautionary tale of what *not* to do in the first forty years. Although, looking back, it's clear Jean and I would never have come together unless our lives had reached that rock bottom. And if you're sitting in life's departure lounge wondering, "Is this all there is?" I hope our story can help change the last chapters of your own journey.

Jean's decision in 2016 to change her medical subspecialty from delivering babies to delivering people to another world proves that it's never too late to set off in a new direction.

Jean and I are wildly in love with each other. We hug often when we're in public; we hold hands incessantly; we become kids again when we see each other after an absence — even just a few hours. We don't talk about it; but we show it.

It's tempting to credit the gods of chance for our meeting and growing together. Luck never gets the credit it deserves, but I believe blind dumb luck plays a very big role in everyone's life. Those of us who are credentialed for success believe these credentials have made all the difference; that we got where we got by working hard and being smart. But if you think back to the exact circumstances of meeting your own life partner, or how you got your first real job, or your first tragedy and how you dealt with it, I'll bet luck was there to turn tomorrow your way. A flick of its finger and a new door can open, or slam shut.

In my own case, if I hadn't been good friends with my doctor, if she wasn't so worried about me to invite me to her cottage for a summer weekend thirty years ago, if I'd decided to join the other guests for a boat ride, if that boat hadn't run out of gas in the middle of Georgian Bay, I would never have met Jean, let alone got to know her in such an odd first-time way. In fact, I think I'd be long dead by now if those circumstances hadn't come together the way they did. Jean reminds me that I'd met her half a dozen times before that meeting via Carolyn Bennett, but she never registered in my brain. I know. Very bad. But lucky.

I don't mean to gush and exaggerate here. Sure, I might have recovered my mental and physical health some other way. I might have met someone else. But as a great friend of mine said after I told him about yet another one of my brushes with death, "How many times has that woman saved your life?"

So what follows is my story, and the story of Jean and me, as told by me.

Before I begin, I just want to say a word about privilege: my late parents would be shocked to hear I was born into it. My father owned a flower shop in Edmonton. But I went to private school and two Ivy League universities, and those worlds rubbed off. I married a doctor. So I've never wanted for anything.

When Covid-19 hit, we fled to our cottage near Penetanguishene. As Covid persisted, that cottage gradually transformed into our home. We could go outside for long walks and not run into a single other soul. We had space and air and a neighbourhood with virtually no Covid for miles around.

So yes, I've been privileged, if that's the right word. A more accurate one would be *lucky*. And that I can enthusiastically agree with, both in life and in love.

It's still so hard to square the person I am today with the little boy growing up in the 1950s. I figure if I can poke at the embers of my childhood and youth, that may cast a glow on how I ended up in the arms of someone whose upbringing also had big holes where love should have been.

Someone once told me that creativity comes from trying to be like everybody else — and failing. I've spent seventy years living all three parts of that last sentence. Looking back, I can tell you it's been thrilling, but also exhausting. Most of all, it's been confusing. How did my life turn out the way it has? How did Jean Marmoreo walk into it and change me — and us — forever? How did we endure against all odds? Because no one, including us, gave us a hope of surviving even dinner and a movie back when we met in 1990. But these two damaged people did go on to connect after an enormous act of chance.

My flaws are out there for all to see. Controlling? Check. Obsessive? Check. Addictive personality? Check.

How did these impulses take hold, fester, and become the drivers of so much of my life? I wasn't abused or raised poor. I had a very comfortable life growing up in Edmonton. I was an only child. My two half-brothers and a half-sister were between fifteen and twenty years older than me.

So, they were gone, really, by the time I arrived.

I was my parent's golden child. My mother was forty-one years old when she had me in 1949 — dangerously old to have your first-born back then — and I suspect I was a bargaining chip in my mom and dad's own coming together. As in "I'll marry you even though you're fifty-five, but I want a child." And so it was that the three of us set off as a family together.

My dad, Donald Ramsay, had been an officer in the 19th Alberta Dragoons during the Second World War, and studied botany at the University of Alberta before taking over the flower shop his father, Walter Ramsay, had founded in 1895. Dad also became the volunteer president of the Edmonton Symphony Orchestra. He'd learned to play the piano as a child, a gift his father gave to him and that he gave to me: a love of classical music and an ease with it from an early age.

My mom, Edith, studied home economics at the University of Alberta. It's tempting to think this was some kind of career-ready training to be an economist. No. It was the science of running your household. No one teaches home ec anymore. But back then, it was what smart young women who wanted to go to university took. It's not that law school or STEM courses were opening doors for them. Back then, many university-educated women didn't work. It just wasn't done.

Edith Ramsay was a wicked bridge player and had an extraordinary charm that captivated people of all ages. When I was in grade six, she would invite the young girls on our street to have tea with her, one on one. They loved being treated as grown-ups. I was in awe of her ability to do that.

But very early in my life, it was clear to me that something was amiss at home.

My mom drank too much and was what they called back then a "social alcoholic."

While I know my dad loved me, he rarely showed it.

He had a hard time saying anything that was both affectionate and clear, and he was awkward about displaying any outward signs of affection. He also avoided the subject of my mom's drinking. He was also stout.

You don't hear the word *stout* much anymore, but it was a nice way to say *fat*. My dad was fat. And old. The other kids' dads weren't fat or old. They played sports. My dad never did. He played a harpsichord, which he built himself.

All of this made me very ashamed. Not only was I born into the wrong family, somehow it was my fault.

Plus, I had my own flaws. The biggest, in my mind at least, was that I was small. I was a good half-foot shorter than the other boys in my class. Six inches in junior high may as well have been a mile. There was nothing subtle about my inadequacy. I equated height with manliness. I'm sure my mom and dad sat me down and told me that being small wasn't a flaw. They likely said it was a special advantage. But I never heard them. For reasons lost in time, and despite years of therapy, I can't recall a single time when anyone picked on me because of my size. Oh, there was the time in grade eight when the dorm bully started beating us up regularly. But when he came to me, he backed off before landing a punch. He knew he needed to pick on someone his own size or he'd lose all credibility as a bully.

All of this said, it was clear to me that we were deficient at our very core, as individuals and as a family. Then again, I was, at most, only eight years old when I first began to sense that things weren't quite as they should be. Being confused about what my parents thought of me, whether they loved me, I instead sought approval from others.

When I played squash as a teen at the local club and a few other members gathered to watch in the gallery, I would catch fire, suddenly playing demonically against my opponent.

This carved out a hole where most people's centre is, which in turn made me terribly sensitive to any of life's highs and lows. Perhaps this was a way to protect myself from the abandonment that I knew deep down would inevitably come. No wonder I became a drug addict.

I don't think I had a choice, really. Either in finding my identity in others, or in veering toward addiction. It wasn't as if I could remove myself from the bundle of anxieties I was becoming, look objectively at my situation, and act accordingly. No child can do this. My parents were the air I breathed. I can't remember one occasion when we actually talked, as in "We need to talk." The three of us, even when I had grown up and they had grown old, lived in bubbles, cut off from one another and the world.

A compounding factor was my parents' huge ambition for me. They wanted me to succeed. Pleasing them became my goal in life. The more I rose, the happier we all were, at least on the surface. Success could redeem their failings and my own.

So my graduating from Princeton was greeted as a redemptive act. I felt it would protect me from life's knocks. I felt it would give me power and control. It would relieve the sense of awkward *almostness* that marked my growing up.

I never talked to my parents about this — are you kidding? — but I'm sure it was true for them, as well.

And yet ... the three of us were intelligent, kind, educated, charming, and outgoing. I've done many extraordinary things, and even a few original ones. I made up for the loneliness that marked my childhood by creating a world for myself in which I would never be alone, where I would always have friends around, lots and lots of them. I once invited a gang of friends up to my tiny cottage north of Toronto when I was in my thirties. We arrived and I unlocked the door and rushed to turn on the music. Rushed. There couldn't be a second's silence between turning the key and turning on the radio. One friend said, "Hey, I thought we came up here for the great outdoors. The quiet." I wasn't offended. I just didn't understand what he was trying to say.

Somewhere in this fear of being alone or enduring silence, I also learned that the only way I was going to get ahead and get the love I craved was to earn it, to perform for it. These days, this is called "contingent love." If I stop performing for you, you'll stop loving me. Or even liking me. So … leading one heli-hiking trip into the Rockies will earn only enough admiration for that year.

I had to do it every year. The terror of what would happen if I ever stopped propelled me to keep running, keep performing, keep succeeding. Years of therapy have made clear the rueful costs of such an unconscious choice. The worst is, of course, the inability to just sit still. In a room. Alone. In the dark. In the silence. And just be. I actually practise doing this now, and it gets easier after the initial terror. But like so many childhood fears driving adult actions, mine are all about fear itself. Just fear. Fear unconnected to much, really. And one blessing is that my memory's fading.

Therapy has also taught me that the wounds you suffer may not be in proportion to the blows your psyche has received. Why am I so paranoid when no one's ever really attacked me? I remember for a month asking a therapist if he thought I'd been sexually abused.

"No."

"Physically abused?"

"No."

"Verbally abused?"

"No."

"Emotionally abused?"

"Of course. Your mother was an alcoholic. A more accurate description would be 'emotionally abandoned.'"

"But my parents adored me!"

"True. Maybe because of that you felt their abandonment all the more."

During my childhood, I was starved for love and stuffed with it. In my twenties and thirties, that terrible need — to search for love with ever-growing panic — drove my life. By the time I was forty, I was desperately unhappy, with a smile frozen on the outside and utter panic taking over on the inside.

So how was it then, that a woman walked into my life and taught me so much about the power of love and its ability to provide redemption?

I guess that's the question this memoir really tries to answer.

I almost died trying to find love. And that love I found has shown me what I've been living for.

1 "So, How Did You Two Meet?"

By the summer of 1990, my cocaine addiction ruled my life. I fought against it, but in the end obeyed its every command.

I'd gone to my doctor a few months earlier to ask for her help. Dr. Carolyn Bennett was also my good friend. Her parents were florists from Toronto; mine were florists from Edmonton. So, naturally, as kids, we'd both been dragged to the same florist conventions every summer, and on the final night of these gatherings, our parents had made us dance with each other. We were eight. Yech!

We parted ways around age twelve, but, oddly, I met her again when she married a school friend of mine, Peter O'Brian. It was 1972, and I was new in Toronto, just starting my first real job. I needed a doctor, and Carolyn was taking patients.

I remember going to her clinic at Bathurst and Bloor for my first appointment. I was wearing a suit and everyone who worked in the clinic was wearing jeans: the doctors, the nurses, the patients, everyone. They were all women, too. *What kind of doctors' office is this?* I thought. Back in 1972, that was a reasonable question.

Over the years, Carolyn and I grew close, and by 1990 the idea of calling her to say I was in trouble with drugs was not as fraught as it could have been.

When Carolyn asked how I planned to stop taking cocaine, I proposed a program of abstinence so ludicrous that I cringe to write about it, even now. My plan was to get my urine tested every week in her clinic's lab in order to prove that I wasn't taking drugs. This makes about as much sense as claiming that wet sidewalks cause rain.

By the third week, I felt so guilty turning up at the lab for my weekly test that I told the technician that I was being considered for a high-security posting in Ottawa and they needed to make sure I was clean before I did the next round of interviews.

Right.

When I initially told Carolyn my plan (which I failed to perfection for the six weeks I did it), she said, "Sure, you can try that," in a voice that implied *Are you kidding me?* "But you might also want to try Cocaine Anonymous or even Alcoholics Anonymous."

I laughed to myself. *Me, go to one of those 12-step programs? I don't live on a park bench. I can beat this on my own. I eat willpower for breakfast. No problem.*

I learned much later that addicts and alcoholics regularly manipulate their family doctors about their addiction.

Saying "My doctor knows" conveys an aura of control when there really is none, and "confessing" my condition to my doctor while at the same time not taking her advice let me still use while thinking I was quitting.

Carolyn was having none of it. One summer day, she called me to ask if I'd like to come up to her family cottage on Georgian Bay for the weekend. There'd be lots of people there, she said, and I might enjoy it. Her real motive, of course, was to keep an eye on me.

I told her I'd love to go. It's important to note here that in mid-addiction, any idea of "I'd love to" do most anything is soon swept away with "I'd hate to." This is the outward manifestation of the split in the addict's brain between "I have to quit" and "I have to use." So, by the time I drove up to the cottage, which was on an island north of Toronto, I was sweating with fear. *What if someone confronts me? What if I start to crave and can't get off the island?* And most of all, *What if I have to actually talk with someone?*

Because by this stage, far from wanting to connect with people, I was desperate to push them away. Turning up at a big summer party was high-risk behaviour for me. But I went because Carolyn would go crazy if I didn't. She might even force me to get help.

It turned out that Carolyn had also invited another of her friends who deserved watching. Jean Marmoreo had been her medical partner for twenty years, and a few months earlier Jean had taken her three children away from their father and filed for divorce. Jean had come to the cottage with her youngest daughter, nine-year-old MaryBeth, and both had chosen to spend the day on a rock off-shore, painting pictures of the island Carolyn's cottage was on, so they were not there when I arrived.

Jean was short and very attractive with a thousand-watt smile. Not that it was flashed in my direction. She seemed to be all business, shepherding her paints and her daughter back to Carolyn's cottage. She certainly didn't meet my standard criteria for an attractive partner: she wasn't tall or drop-dead gorgeous, though she was blonde.

Don't even ask why these all had to do with appearance. They're a measure of the stunning lack of depth in my relationships with women, and tell you something about why I'd had such a large number of short-term relationships.

On my way north, I'd remembered I should bring a gift to my hostess. As there were no florists on the rocks of Georgian Bay, I popped into a convenience store and picked up bags of candy bars, gum, potato chips, and pretzels, which I proudly presented to Carolyn when I arrived.

She looked askance and said, "The kids will love you."

Exactly. I could be a hero to them and at the same time satisfy my huge cravings for sugar and salt.

Later that afternoon, Carolyn got a phone call from Doug Barrett, the neighbour one island over. Doug had just bought a brand-new powerboat and wanted us all to join him for a test ride. He told her he'd be over to pick us up in ten minutes.

Did I want to go? Not a chance. Doug Barrett was a good friend of mine, and I knew he'd sense there was something wrong with me, so I opted to stay at the cottage with the kids while all the other grown-ups joined him. All except Jean and her daughter, of course, who were still off painting on the rock. Doug, Carolyn, and the gang said they'd be back in an hour, and off they headed across the water. They were soon just a speck on the horizon.

One hour passed. Then two. *Hmmm ... they must be having fun out there*, I thought. By seven thirty, Jean and her daughter had returned to the cottage. "Where is everyone?" she asked, realizing I was the only adult there.

"On Doug Barrett's new boat. They said they'd be back a while ago."

"We'd better make the burgers," she said, opening the fridge.

All the kids were playing outside, leaving Jean and me alone in the kitchen. We started getting dinner ready, though my skills in that department were at that time fairly non-existent.

I introduced myself as a patient of Carolyn's.

"I know who you are," she said.

Years later, Jean would tell me that we'd actually met half a dozen times since I'd become a patient of their practice; I just never remembered her. Jean also told me that Carolyn had asked if she could give me a ride up north that weekend. Carolyn was worried that I would cancel at the last minute or kill myself on the highway if I drove high. Jean had told her, "Bob Ramsay is mad, bad, and dangerous to know. No thank you."

And thus began our relationship.

But I knew none of this that Saturday evening on Georgian Bay. In fact, Jean seemed quite civil as we prepared the hamburger patties for dinner. I got the sense she knew about my addiction, which turned out to be a relief. I could never have told her the truth, but at least I didn't have to lie.

I found out she'd recently separated from her husband, so I asked her the same impertinent question I'd asked scores of women over the years (and still do): "What kind of man are you looking for?" (Which assumed that looking for a man was something they even thought of.)

I never asked in order to get a woman to say, "A man like you, Bob!" I was just curious. And the more I asked that question, the more I was taken with the responses, or at least their sameness. Then and now, I know lots of single women between the ages of forty and sixty-five. Most are highly accomplished, many with successful careers; few, if any, are victims.

So, when I asked about the kind of man they'd like to go out with, I used to expect them to say something like "An apex predator like me!" Or at least, "Someone smart and accomplished." But no, I truly never got any replies like that.

It was always "I'm not looking for a rocket scientist. I just want someone who's kind and can make me laugh."

Really? This struck me as perversely subservient. Then again, I knew a woman who once was the assistant deputy attorney general in charge of prosecuting major crimes in Ontario. She was tough on every front. Except she was going out with a guy who owned a restaurant, and every night she'd wait at home for him to call (or not) to tell her she could join him for a nightcap at the bar or for dinner. How odd, I thought. I called her "Killer by Day, Puddle by Night."

So, when I idly asked Jean the same question, I was expecting the answer that virtually every other woman had given me. But instead she said, "I'm looking for a man who's got a lot of money, a lot of power, and who loves sex."

Uh ... what did she say?

"Really?" I choked out. I thought of saying "I'm your guy!" but that would have been dead wrong on three fronts. Instead, I kept my mouth shut and thought, *What an odd woman.* She scared the hell out of me.

Just before it got dark, we heard a noise down by the dock. The boat had returned. As everyone disembarked, we heard the whole sad story. Doug Barrett had misjudged how much fuel the boat needed and they'd run out of gas in the middle of Georgian Bay.

Everyone was tired and the several who had stuck their heads into the engine bay were sick from breathing in the fumes. No one wanted any dinner. They just wanted to go to bed.

So there Jean and I were, alone, having made two dozen hamburgers, of which only half had been eaten by the kids, who didn't go on the boat ride.

Oddly, I don't remember another word of what either of us talked about that night, and neither does she. It's tempting to say we talked all night. We didn't.

But I do know that a few days later, I picked up the phone and called her at her clinic and asked if she'd like to go to a movie.

At first there was only silence at the other end. Then "A movie? With you? When?"

"Uh … how about tonight? Or tomorrow?" It's not as if I had a full dance card.

"Tonight? No, I can't do that." Another long silence.

How many ways did I screw this up?

"Look … I'm going camping," she finally said. "I'll be back in a couple of weeks. Call me then if you want."

That's a yes, I thought. *She just said yes — kind of.*

"Okay, I'll call you in two weeks."

But I didn't, because a week later my friends intervened on me and I found myself nine hundred miles away at Talbott Recovery Center in Atlanta, Georgia.

We'd never even gone out for coffee. The hook was in, though, in both of us.

2   *Dad* Is a Four-Letter Word

Since I grew up as, effectively, an only child, my only companions for most meals were my mom and dad.

One night at dinner when I was nine or ten, the phone rang in the kitchen. I ran to get it. It was for my dad. I held out the phone on the long cord that just reached to the door. My parents could see the phone, but they couldn't see me. "It's for you," I said, from back in the kitchen.

"For who?" said my dad.

"For you," I said. I was seized with fear.

"For me?" said my father, growing impatient. I could barely speak now.

"Yes, yes, it's for you."

A little annoyed, he got up from the table to take the phone. "Then why can't you just say so?"

I went back to the table. My mother looked at me oddly. I was red with shame.

I couldn't say the word *Dad*.

What drove this odd, crippling fear? Did he beat me? No. Abuse me in other ways? Never. Back in 1959 when this happened, my father was fifty-five years old, quite old to have such a young son.

I'd describe his demeanour as *formal* — in the language of that time — perhaps *distant* would be more accurate in the language of today.

What stunned me about this incident was that I didn't know until that moment just how afraid of my father I was. When you can't even say, "Dad," and instead are reduced to saying, "It's for *you*," that speaks to a much deeper problem. Was I afraid that if I said, "Dad," he would say, "No, I'm not your dad!" or "Yes, I'm your dad, but no, I don't love you"? Not consciously. But at some level, I realize that I was always anxious about what most kids and their parents view as unconditional. I also think I was afraid of being embarrassed. Since I'd never called my dad *Dad*, the fact that I was on the verge of doing it for the first time at the age of nine made me cringe. This dread of not knowing how to do what everyone else does, and not knowing how to learn to — and then faking it — would spill out in all kinds of negative ways when I grew up.

And on that night, I was exposed, not just as an imposter, but as incompetent. I had failed at being normal, and that failure would twist and turn me for much of my life.

3 Short Kid. Sharp Words

One obvious way I felt I was not normal as I was growing up was that I was short. At five foot three, I still am today.

I got into an argument with my therapist on this point a few years back when he asked why I thought I was so driven. "Oh, that's easy. Because I'm short, and from Edmonton."

"No, you're not," he said, smiling. He was going over old ground with me.

"Pardon?"

"Yes, you're from Edmonton. No, you're not short."

"Of course I'm short."

"No, you're not."

"Look. I'm five foot three. I … am … short!"

"You just think you are."

"True. But I also *am*."

"No."

"Yes!"

He laughed. Whatever reality he wanted me to embrace, it's clear to anyone with eyes that I have a huge desire to be noticed and taken seriously. I couldn't change my height, so literally standing out would be impossible. But if I couldn't be seen, I could be heard.

Looking back, a big part of my life has been my struggle to do that. I have no idea if this is because my mother, the "social alcoholic," wasn't there for her crying baby, or because my father was a man who deeply loved me but lacked the ability to show it.

My own rage at not being heard drove me so hard that it's defined huge parts of my life. I write for a living. I speak for a living. I teach other people how to speak and write for a living. Given my need and drive to be heard, how was it that I developed a stammer so bad I would hide from people for fear they would hear me and run away?

It's little wonder I was mesmerized by the final scene in the film *The King's Speech*, when George VI spits out "I have a voice!" after finally conquering his stammer.

When I was around twelve, I had an odd kind of stammer. I was fine talking with another person and maybe with two. But any number beyond that and words failed me. My mouth turned to marbles. I was also tongue-tied when I felt I was being put on the spot, when someone asked me a direct question, or when that someone was an adult.

I couldn't hide in one- or two-word comebacks. I couldn't deflect with a clever line. I was being judged, and my inability to start a word, let alone finish one, told the world I was not to be taken seriously.

About that time, my parents noticed that something was wrong, and sent me to a speech therapist. I remember the very kind grey-haired lady who asked me to read slowly from *Grimms' Fairy Tales*. I went to her only five or six times and I have no idea what she told my parents my problem was. But they never talked about my stammer; instead, it was discussed as an issue with "reading aloud." That way, no one need be embarrassed. No one had a defective child, or was one. It was just a matter of learning how to read aloud better.

I tried to fix my stammer when I was sent to boarding school, where I stayed, with great happiness, for six years from grades eight through thirteen. At Trinity College School in the midsixties, we attended chapel every day and twice on Sunday. During each service, one student had to get up in front of the entire school — three hundred boys — and read the daily lesson from the Bible. I knew I couldn't escape it.

I also couldn't do what I'd become very clever at, which was quickly substituting a word I could say whenever I ran up against one I couldn't climb to the second syllable of. Stammerers become very good at this quick-switch, and that may be one reason I find it easy years later to come up with three words to describe one thing when I'm writing.

But you don't get to substitute your own words when you're reading the Bible. What I did do is memorize the lesson — it was just five minutes long. That way, at least I knew what was coming.

But all of that didn't save me. I was a red-faced, sputtering teenager, whose agony was shared by the teachers in chapel and quietly laughed at by some of the students.

It wasn't just ironic that I couldn't do the one thing I was compelled to — "I have a voice!" — I couldn't tell anymore whether my stammer forced me to work even harder to be heard, or whether my need to be heard was so desperate that even my stammer couldn't stop it.

But it's not even that simple.

In my first month at Trinity, I tried out for the junior school soccer team. I was a real outsider, coming from Edmonton where no one ever came from. I'd also never played soccer before. But I was quick.

One day during tryouts, the ball was passed to me and I took a shot. The goalie caught it in his arms, but I, rather than turning back because he was going to throw it to one of his teammates, rushed the goalie and kicked the ball out of his hands and into the net. He lay on the ground, winded.

"Goooooooooooooooaaaaaaaaalll!"

No. Not a goal. It is apparently against the rules to touch an opposing goalie when he has the ball, let alone kick him in the chest to dislodge it. Everyone knows that. Except me, because I didn't know the rules of the game.

So, when I turned to accept the adoring cheers of my teammates, all I got was their stunned silence, and the coach yelling, "Ramsay, what the hell are you doing?"

I didn't understand. I'd scored. I hadn't slowed down when he caught the ball. I'd practically thrown myself at him. The goalie picked himself up, called me an asshole, and we carried on.

Later, in the locker room, he came over to me, twisted my shirt into a knot at my neck, and barked, "If you ever fucking touch me again, I will kill you."

I was terrified. That night at dinner, my terror grew. I realized that he and I were assigned to the same dining table for all our meals for the next two months. Oh crap. Bullying three times a day?

Yes, but not by him, it turned out.

It didn't take long for word to spread through the entire junior school how this tiny know-nothing kid from out west had kicked one of the most senior kids hard in the chest to score a goal. But this wasn't just any bigger, older kid I'd kicked. He came from one of Canada's most famous families.

His great-grandfather had practically built the railroad out west in the late 1800s.

I was dead.

But, oddly, he steered clear of me at the dining table. I think he was so tall and I was so small that any overt act of aggression on his part would look unfair. I was to use this idea of "too small to fail" to my advantage years later. Besides, he was a year older than me — an infinity in junior high — so, I wasn't worth even looking at.

It was into this silence that I decided to poke the bear a bit. At breakfast, I would say something slightly cutting to the boy beside him. My tormentor would be drawn in, and I'd prod him directly, but not in a way he could take offence to. I quickly learned to use sarcasm — saying one thing and meaning another — as a kind of barbed code that only he understood. Again, he didn't push back. He wasn't all that smart, and words weren't his thing, so I kept pushing. Over the next two months, I moved from being careful and indirect to ... well, to making his life so miserable that he asked to be transferred to another table before our natural rotation out.

Against all odds, I had won.

I realized I could use words to beat people up. Use words to gain control of my life.

So how was it that, at the very same time, and for the next five years, I was also crippled by a stammer?

4 Salad Days, Green in Judgment

From that moment on, I thrived at Trinity, all six years of it from grades eight through thirteen. I threw myself into everything with enormous energy, though with hardly any thought. During my final year, in 1968, I was the captain of three varsity teams — soccer, squash, and cricket — and was the head of the drama club, the head of the choir, and a member of the debating team.

And by my final year at Trinity, I had also found my voice through writing. It began when, for a grade thirteen midterm English exam, I had to write a 250-word essay — a staggering number of words,

I thought at the time. Rather than starting it with a high-schooler's clunky construct of "The purpose of this essay is to contrast Hamlet's [whatever]," I instead wrote, "Hamlet was blind in more ways than one." I continued with this irreverent style until I was done. I don't know why I decided to veer off the road this way. Maybe it was because I felt good and wanted to show off. Whatever the reason, when I got my paper back three days later, the teacher had written "A+. A new and sprightly style. Excellent!"

It's odd that I can still remember this entire event in minute detail: the May sun shining onto my desk; the old attic-like classroom; the fact that my English teacher was distant in ways my father was; the word *sprightly*, which sounded to me musty and Victorian.

The day before graduation, a much-loved teacher came over to bid me farewell. "Ramsay," he said, because we were only known by our last names by staff, "I hope you enter university with the same enthusiasm and energy as you've done here."

Energy? Enthusiasm? I didn't know what he meant by that. What anyone could see about me in thirty seconds, I seemed blind to. It also offers a clue to how rudderless I was beneath all that frantic paddling.

But I'd done well in school. I was a jock. I was an arts guy.

I applied to a number of Ivy League universities and got into Princeton. It seems I was a "student-athlete." Their squash coach even sent me a handwritten letter encouraging me to attend. They'd just built a big new gym with forty-seven squash courts. There had only been two squash courts at Trinity.

That's all it took to get me onto the Port Authority bus in New York City for the one-hour ride to Princeton, New Jersey, where I would live and study for the next four years.

I was lucky. Those too were salad days. Luckier still that my parents paid the entire shot for my time there, at whatever unspoken sacrifice to their own plans.

My freshman year was like my six years at Trinity, an all-male experience.

But in 1969, Princeton made the momentous decision to admit women for the first time since its founding in 1746. In that first year there were 130 women in a university of 4,000 undergraduates. I fell in love with one of them.

My relationship with Jacqui began in my senior year and just petered out. To say our relationship was doomed from the start implies that it had a natural arc with a passionate beginning, rising conflict in the middle, and a lot of yelling at the end. Not true here.

She was going out with a math professor when we met — a domineering, charismatic older man who'd been married before — in the days when it was okay for professors to date students, I guess. By the time I graduated in June of 1972, Jacqui and I were still seeing each other — or rather were having an affair, because her math professor had come roaring back, sending us into furtiveness. We made fleeting promises to stay in touch as she headed home to Chicago and I headed back to Toronto. The sheer vagueness of our relationship spoke to the deep fear I had of getting involved in one — and the deep need, as well. Looking back, I'm amazed at how passive I was throughout.

This was my first real relationship and to have it be a fight to the finish ... well, that would be more than I could handle. So I did what I would do often in the years to come. I just moved on, hoping that the next shiny object would be more permanent than the last.

Jacqui was the full extent of my experience with women by the time I started my first job in Toronto, as a speech writer for Ontario premier Bill Davis. Not much of a grounding in healthy relationships with the opposite sex.

Over the next fifteen years, between when I was twenty-five and the day after I turned forty on August 22, 1989, my work life and personal life were frantic, chaotic, and stuffed down into my psyche so I couldn't feel a thing. But my stammer, long repressed, came back. I remember my boss in the Premier's Office, Clare Westcott, would ask me to call someone in a government department to get some crucial information. I couldn't get through "Mr. Smith, this is Bob Ramsay calling from the Premier's Office. Clare Westcott asked me to call." So I would find the person's office address, show up unannounced, hand my Premier's Office business card to the secretary, and say that I just happened to be in the area and could I have a few words with the boss.

An eternal type of bad boy is the one who can't break off a relationship he's not serious about (and likely never was), either because he's only in it for the sex, or he's afraid of confrontation, or honesty scares him even more.

That was me in the 1970s.

I'd been having an affair with my business partner for a few months. She was serious about me. But I was proving I could break the first rule of the office and break someone's heart with no ill effects to either. After three months of feeble excuses about not having time to be with her but having time to be with other women (often clients we shared), she walked into my office one day and said, "We're having dinner tonight." And before I could cook up an excuse, she dropped the hammer. "And we're going to go to my place and order in and we're going to talk about you and me. See you at seven." Then she walked out.

Even I couldn't call up at seven and cancel. I wasn't a complete *cad*. So, I prepared to meet my doom. I remember not having a clue what I'd say. I certainly didn't think that coming clean would actually make us both feel better.

She lived in a downtown high-rise and the doorman rang me in at seven fifteen. I took the elevator up, knocked on her door, said hi, and we then went through five minutes of agonizing small talk. She told me she'd ordered Chinese and it would be there at seven thirty.

Precisely at seven thirty, her buzzer rang. She turned to me and said, "You'll want to pay for the food and the cab." She went back into the kitchen to get some plates.

"Sure, okay."

A minute later, I heard the elevator stop on her floor, followed quickly by a knock on the door. I opened it up and ... standing there holding a big bag of Chinese food was an old friend from high school, Tony Rowley.

We both looked shocked to see each other.

"Tony ... what are you doing here?!"

"Bob Ramsay ... wow, it's been a long time!"

My "girlfriend" came to the doorway. "What's going on?"

"Meet my great friend from school, Tony Rowley. Tony, come on in and join us for dinner."

"Are you sure?"

"Absolutely! It will be great to catch up ... Don't worry, I'll pay for your time off ..."

Tony stayed for dinner, turning Chinese for two into Chinese for three. He must have sensed something was wrong and left after an hour of false heartiness all round: me constantly asking him to regale us with stories of school days and him trying to make driving a cab sound like a typical career choice for a graduate of Cambridge.

After Tony left, my hostess was so disgusted with us both that she said, "Just go. Please. Go now."

I did.

The Cheshire grin on my face was with me all the way home that night and in the office the next morning.

Through sheer luck, I had escaped the noose.

One month later, she left the company for a big job at the CBC — I hadn't escaped the truth.

A few times during those fifteen years I had relationships with women that lasted maybe three months. But they would never last longer than that, either because we were entirely unsuited, or, more frequently, because I would flee. I was terrified of getting close to someone, of their really knowing me. I also just couldn't sit still.

In those days, I would date tall blonde women. They were never bimbos: no, no, I wasn't one of *those* men. In fact, the women I went out with had to be smart and accomplished. Again, I was blind to what everyone in my world could see: that my relationship with women was, in the words of a friend, "deeply surface."

All I can say is that, because of my high level of energy, because of my talents, because of my social skills, it took a very long time for the fragile foundations holding me up to collapse.

But collapse they did.

It happened on a weekend bicycle trip I'd organized in 1989 for two dozen friends in Port Hope, an hour east of Toronto. After a thirty-mile bike ride on the Saturday, we all met at a restaurant in town for dinner. Our group was split into tables of four, and I no-ticed that Linda, the woman I'd been going out with but had never really broken up with, though I wanted to, was sitting at a table with our hosts, David and Anita Blackwood, whose garden was our base camp for the cycling expeditions. Also seated at that table was another woman, Julia, who I'd gone for dinner with recently and planned to end the weekend with.

Well, Anita Blackwood turned to this new friend and asked her how she knew me, to which she replied, "Oh, I'm going out with him."

This prompted Linda to say, "You are? So am I."

I found this out because Anita told me afterward. But I didn't need her translation to know that, at that precise moment, my goose was cooked. Their entire table looked over at me with utter contempt. Linda got up and left, never to return.

By Sunday morning, everyone in the group knew what had happened. I was shunned by all the women on the bike ride.

As it turns out, I had given my apartment in Toronto over to a friend who was visiting from Vancouver. I had been certain I wouldn't need it until Monday because I assumed I'd be in Julia's bed on Sunday night. So, I had to book a room at the Hotel Ibis on Jarvis Street. When I arrived there around nine Sunday night, I parked my car out on the street and went inside. When I went to get the car on Monday morning, it had been towed. Something terrible had happened that weekend and my impounded car was just a symptom of a much worse malady. I wasn't sure quite what it was, but I was still busy defending myself, saying, "I never slept with her. What's the big deal?" But even I, in all my blindness, could see I couldn't carry on like this. I had to do something.

Or rather, something had to be done. I've switched into the passive voice here because I had no ability to consciously decide anything.

Rather, a decision seems to have been made to pick up the phone and call my doctor and friend, Carolyn Bennett. I didn't bother telling her what had happened, I just blurted out, "I just can't seem to sustain a relationship with a woman. I don't know why. I think I may need to talk to someone." Then I started sobbing.

Carolyn immediately said she'd find someone for me to talk to. I sensed she'd been waiting for this call for a long time. She called back an hour later to inform me I had my first appointment with a therapist the next week.

I was relieved but asking for help was all still so alien and shameful, so fearful and threatening.

Maybe that's why, just one month later, the day after my very big and public fortieth birthday party, my life didn't take a turn for the better; in fact, it got much worse.

5 When the Train Runs You Over, It's Not the Caboose That Kills You

My fortieth birthday party was a celebration befitting my view of myself. Two hundred people attended a dinner in the old Molson brewery in downtown Toronto. There were speeches lauding my frenetic energy, my affability, and my love of making connections. On the eve of turning forty, I was running a thriving communications agency and all seemed well, except on the personal front.

Arts guru Peter Herrndorf paused in his speech that birthday night to ask, "Would all the women who have slept with Bob Ramsay please stand up." And every woman in the room did just that. I was both thrilled and mortified. Was I *that* obvious?

But the bigger question I asked myself was, were they laughing with me or at me? That essential paranoia that had protected me from the slings and arrows that never existed was now beginning to plague me. My thank-you speech that night reflected my fragile view of myself. I somehow thought that saying someone's got to be the court jester, so why not me, would elevate me in the eyes of my friends. Their applause was muted.

Here I was being feted by masses of good friends and I still didn't believe their affection was real; or if it was, that it would be there come morning.

The day after my birthday celebration, I was standing outside my office on Bloor Street enjoying a glorious summer day, when a man I vaguely recognized came up to me. "Bob Ramsay! How are you, man?"

I hadn't seen this guy in years. He was a building contractor and the former boyfriend of a woman I knew well. The last time I'd seen him was years earlier on a ski trip in Utah. I remember he spent nearly all his time on the phone and always spoke outside of earshot. I learned later that he was really a drug dealer who got himself arrested and sentenced to a long prison term in the United States. But somehow, he'd finagled a transfer to a Canadian prison and was now out on parole. He was an odd character, part professional liar and part stand-up guy.

I asked what he was up to.

"Oh … stuff, I guess. You?"

"Well, I just had my fortieth birthday last night."

"Oh, wow. Congratulations!"

After we talked for another few minutes, he said, "Look, I've got a birthday present for you. Let's go up to your office and I'll give it to you."

Upstairs, with my office door safely closed, he pulled out an envelope with four grams of cocaine in it. "Here. It's not every day a guy gets to be forty."

I didn't really use cocaine then, but I thought that it was awfully generous of him. And besides, given that he was a drug dealer, I'm sure he didn't have to spend what I would to get it. I thanked him and wished him well and he left.

I put the envelope in my desk drawer and forgot about it for two months.

But one night in October, I was working late in the office, frantically trying to meet a deadline. I remembered I'd taken cocaine years ago and the friend who gave it to me promised it would not only help me concentrate, it would help me write better and clearer.

Hmm … I thought. I guess snorting a line or two could only make me more productive. Cocaine is not at all like cannabis, which makes you feel stoned, or alcohol, which makes you feel relaxed. Coke makes you feel "clear." Snort a couple of lines and you will feel confident, in control, charming, and articulate. Or maybe not. Some people feel jittery, their hearts beating too fast. Others "feel nothing."

But for the most part, coke puts you in charge. Until, like all mood-altering substances, it doesn't.

By December, I was snorting a gram a day, which is pretty much the equivalent of drinking a bottle of Scotch a day. I would drive while high and was once stopped for going too slowly in a thirty kilometre an hour zone. At the office, my staff were leaving, the company imploding.

As with all addictions, mine came in three phases. At first, it was all good, all the time. I was bright and sharp and, in fact, I would write better. I could also talk … and talk and talk at parties. I was big and strong and smart and sexy.

After a time, though, it stopped just being all good and became bad, too. That's the thing about cocaine. Not only does it speed you up, it accelerates your decline and fall. One reason is money. A bottle of wine may cost fifteen dollars, but a gram of coke costs $150. Cocaine is also much more addictive than alcohol. So when you read about alcoholics leaving their families destitute, coke addicts just do it ten times faster. That's the spending money part.

The earning money part is much the same. While a little cocaine can make you very focused and productive, for too many people a little cocaine quickly becomes a lot of cocaine. You're now too jumpy to focus, too edgy to have a rational conversation with anyone.

My business manager told me she knew right away when one of her clients was on coke. Their expenses — especially "cash" — rose instantly and their revenues fell like a stone.

By March I'd stopped making payments on my mortgage. My clients had all walked away, tired of my constantly missed deadlines.

I would never be high with other people; only alone. And as I cut myself off more and more from the people who sustained me, I would spend my nights alone at home pretending to write. It would go like this: Lock all the doors. Tape black plastic sheeting to the slits in the curtains so no light could get through. Turn down the ringer on the phone because the noise of a call would send me into a panic. Start typing. Take more coke. Get so jittery that I couldn't type any longer. Try to write with a pen. Give up. Make lists of what I planned to do tomorrow and with my life. Once I even made a list of ways I was going to get revenge on a surly neighbour.

By the end, nothing was good and everything was bad. To get some sleep, I would drink a bottle of wine in bed, hoping that would bring me down. I stopped eating and lost weight. Yet, at the same time, I thought if I could jog for a couple of miles a day, my health would improve. So, I'd run, but drop in to a coffee shop along my route and ask if I could use the bathroom. I'd snort a couple of lines, then head out again. Don't ask me what that did to my heart.

6   In Treatment

Every law society and college of physicians and surgeons in North America knows about Talbott. It's where they send their impaired members. As does Major League Baseball, many airlines, and some churches and armed forces.

The threat of their taking away your licence to perform surgery or fly planes if you don't complete their treatment program is one factor in Talbott's low dropout rate. You're always free to leave, but you'll be barred from your livelihood if you do. I faced no such sanction, but I knew that if I went AMA — Against Medical Advice — I'd be back on drugs.

Talbott combines aggressive individual and group therapy with the principles of Alcoholics Anonymous. This strikes some people as a contradiction. Medicine is about science. AA is about faith; there's no science to it at all.

AA and its many related groups, such as Cocaine Anonymous, Overeaters Anonymous, Gamblers Anonymous, and even Clutterers Anonymous, are called 12-step programs because they ask their members to take twelve steps to get better. These range from admitting you're powerless over alcohol (or drugs, hoarding, gambling) to admitting *all* the bad things you did while under its influence and making amends to the people you've hurt. The twelve steps of Alcoholics Anonymous were written in 1925 and haven't changed since. The first time I heard the twelve steps, I thought, *This stuff is so dated. And what is all this about a Higher Power? When I get out of here, I'm going to call their office in New York and tell them I'll rewrite the steps for them — for nothing.* I cringe at that memory. Was I really that cocky and in denial? It seems I was.

AA has also come under fire recently because many people don't succeed in getting sober through it. To which I say, "Well, it's worked for me." It's also hard to really create valid data on anything if your members can join just by turning up, or leave and go to a different AA group, or leave and never return, all without giving even their names, let alone paying any money.

One other reason Talbott works is that it's long-term treatment. Time alone plays a large role in getting well. I was there four months. Relapsing anesthesiologists, whose *profession* is to dispense drugs to knock people out, regularly stay for a year. Talbott wants to be ultra-sure we won't relapse — and despite all this, of course, some of us do, over and over again.

Our days were filled with one-on-one therapy and group therapy. The latter is important because a big part of addiction is denial.

Most people who have cancer don't say to the world "I don't have cancer." Or heart failure. Or a broken leg. But a defining quality of people who take mood-altering substances too much is their insistence that they are not taking too much, that they're not hurting anyone, that they can stop any time. In fact, I'd say denial is the prime symptom of addiction, along with insane impulsivity. Otherwise, why would people who have lost so much in their lives because of their drug and alcohol use insist that things are fine, or that what cost them their job and their marriage and their freedom was something else? We are blind to what ails us.

But the people around us can see what we refuse to acknowledge. This is one reason why group therapy works for alcoholics and addicts. Others can see what we addicts can't.

The first step in recovery at Talbott is like doing your First Step in AA, in which we admit that we are powerless over alcohol and that our lives have become unmanageable. About two weeks into the program, a therapist will ask you to prepare to give your First Step. At Talbott, that meant sitting in a group of two dozen other fellow newcomers and reading your confession of how your addiction started and progressed, who you hurt and how, and what the consequences were.

In other words, all the bad news, especially the stuff you were afraid to confess to *anyone* before, all at once. Reading time: forty-five minutes. Feedback time: fifteen minutes.

I'd sat through enough of these sessions since my arrival to hear the most dreadful tales. Like the doctor who'd relapsed on cocaine after he left treatment and lived in dread of "random urines," which he was called to give once every few days by his Impaired Physicians Board. He knew if he was caught, he'd lose his licence. So, he peed clean when he knew there was no cocaine in his system and stored that urine in a bottle that he would have on him at all times during the day. He also carried a hypodermic needle so he could inject the clean sample into his urine stream via a "supra-pubic-injection," which he'd have to perform incredibly fast in a hospital washroom.

Or the California doctor, also a cocaine addict, whose twin brother, also a doctor, was killed in a car accident back east. The family was furious at the surviving brother's failure to turn up to the funeral of his twin, because he was so stoned he couldn't get on the plane. But they sent him some of his brother's ashes, anyway, so he could cast them into the ocean near where they had grown up. Thus my fellow Talbott patient kept the ashes in an urn on his fireplace mantle. He had decided this would be a good place to store his cocaine, in a plastic bag.

Who would look there? Well, the bag leaked, and the ashes and the cocaine got all mixed together. Which is how my friend ended up snorting his brother.

When I heard stories like this, I would say, "Wow, not me!" To which the Talbott therapists would smile and say, "Not yet."

When I arrived on May 11, 1990, Talbott put me in detox for seventy-two hours, which they do to everyone who arrives. Coming off my two-gram-a-day cocaine habit, I didn't get the shakes, or throw up, or scratch my arms bloody. What I did was sleep. I also started to eat again, which I'd largely given up when I was using, since cocaine suppresses your appetite.

Once I moved out of detox and in with my roommates, I was caught up in the busyness of doing new things sixteen hours a day. I'd always been a novelty-seeker and this was a feast for me. There were people to meet, therapists to tell my story to, groups to talk in (but mainly keep my mouth shut and learn from). I needed to figure out how to function in this new environment, how to do well in the program, and how to "graduate" and get out of there as quickly as possible.

During my first week there, at an all-campus meeting, all the newbies were asked to stand and state their names, where they're from, what they do for a living, and what their drug of choice is. One patient said she was a Delta pilot, but that she wasn't an alcoholic; she was just there for a seventy-two-hour assessment.

After the half-dozen of us had checked in, the therapist running the meeting said, "Anyone else?" Another patient stood up and said, "My name's Bill; I'm here on the two hundred and sixteenth day of my seventy-two-hour assessment."

Hmmm. Maybe this wasn't going to be as easy as I thought.

There was a guy in our therapist group who got out in ninety days, but for most patients it was four to six months.

Two weeks in, I was still very tired, and as the haze started to lift on my drug use, I was also growing sad at the devastation I'd caused. I was thinking mainly of myself, of course. I'd lost my business because of cocaine; I was pretty sure I was going to lose my home; and Jean, the new and very different woman I'd been going out with, well, such was the depth of my self-knowledge, that I thought we'd just be able to pick up where we left off when I got home.

In one of our biweekly "house" meetings, where the twelve of us on our apartment floor got together, my roommate Dan said he wondered when I was going to get serious about my recovery. I was shocked. I had no idea what he was talking about. I was speaking up in therapy groups and meetings; I was speaking frankly with my therapist. I was doing the program.

When I told Dan and my roommates that I'd never felt sadder in all my life, they all laughed. *They. All. Laughed.* At me.

"But Bob," said Ted the priest, looking at Dan and Jon, "all we see is this happy-go-lucky guy who's witty and pretty manic."

I was crushed by their judgment. How could they not see my anguish? I learned later it was because I simply couldn't show my pain to them.

My addictionologist, Dr. Frederick Veit, suggested that I should do my First Step a week from then. I jumped at the chance. I was getting impatient listening to other patients' gruesome tales, if only because they kept me from telling mine and moving on to the rest of treatment, especially to the stage referred to as "Mirror Image," which begins about halfway through your treatment at Talbott.

Mirror Image is an eight-week or longer internship in which you work as a junior counsellor at one of the many treatment centres in Greater Atlanta. Half a dozen Talbott patients work six hours a day at each centre, doing medical and psychological intakes and leading group-therapy sessions. Generally, once you'd done your time in Mirror Image, you were put on the track for "Re-Entry" — and home.

Here I hadn't even done my First Step and I was already counting the days till I would get out — out to do what, I wasn't quite sure: I'd left a stack of chaos back home. At least I was feeling a lot better physically. I was putting on weight and even running a mile a day around the cinder track beside the apartment complex.

So, when the time came to give my First Step, I was convinced I was ready. I wrote it all out, mentioning everyone my addiction had hurt. This included my previous girlfriend, who had said on our first date that she would never go out with an addict because her last boyfriend was one and had almost ruined her life. I'd nodded and laughed. Also on my list were my late parents, who would wonder what their Golden Child was doing in a place like this and how I had failed the magnificent promise they had made possible for me.

I remember making sure it sounded like a well-crafted opinion piece, with a grabber of an opening and a twist at the end. I was happy to be given the chance to show the other patients what a good writer I was.

The night before you give your First Step, you have to show it to the therapist who heads the sessions the next day. I gave mine to Tom Power, an old southern gentleman, and waited for twenty minutes outside his office while he reviewed it.

He finally opened the door and handed it back to me. "You're good to go tomorrow morning."

"It's okay?"

"It's very well written," he told me.

"Thank you!"

As I left, my heart leapt with hope. *I'm out of here!*

7 My First Step

The next morning, when I walked to the large group-therapy room at Talbott, twenty-four chairs were laid out in a circle. My roommate Dan had walked with me from our apartment and sat beside me in the circle. Tom, the therapist who I'd shown my First Step presentation to the previous evening, wasn't there. In his place was Carol Bowers, who we patients all called Nurse Ratched, because she looked, spoke, and acted like the woman who made Jack Nicholson's life miserable in *One Flew Over the Cuckoo's Nest*. She told us Tom had been called away and that she'd be leading the session.

There's a strict protocol to your First Step. No matter how ragged or how many gulps and tears, you get to read your entire story with no interruptions. It's your chance to get everything out, and you have up to forty-five minutes to do that. When you're done, anyone who wants to comment on what you've said is free to do so, but they — including the therapist — have to connect what they've just heard from you with their own experience. As in "When you said you're a surgeon and you can't get a job in a McDonald's, that reminded me of when I had to sleep on the couch of my grown children because I was homeless." Then, when the session was done, everyone in the room would move to the speaker and give him or her a hug, and we'd all leave together.

The therapist has to give you a pass on your First Step for you to move forward in treatment, but I'd only heard of a couple of people in years past who had to do theirs over.

When you're confessing your innermost secrets and shame of your addiction, forty-five minutes can feel like an awfully long time. I've never heard of a Catholic confessing for three-quarters of an hour before the priest says a word. But I had no trouble talking for that time, no trouble at all.

When I was done, I was a bit teary, to be sure, and frankly exhausted from the effort. I looked up at the assembled group and asked for feedback.

Not one person raised their hand. I scanned the room from right to left. Still no one. Not even Nurse Ratched. My gaze then came to rest on my roommate sitting in the chair beside me, there to provide moral support. He was leaning back, his arms folded across his chest.

"Mr. Ramsay …"

"Yes?" I replied to Nurse Ratched.

"That was the worst First Step I've heard in my twenty years at Talbott. You need to leave here and go out and use some more and come back when you're ready to get clean and sober."

I was stunned. *Worst First Step? What is she saying?! Hadn't Tom last night said it was "very well written"?*

Nurse Ratched then asked me what I did for a living.

What a strange question, I thought. She knew what I did. I'd told her when she inquired in a group during my first week.

"I'm … I'm a writer."

"Well, you are a terrible writer!" Her jaw and eyes seemed set in stone.

I'd had enough. This was a farce. If she wanted me to leave, I would. She didn't know what she was doing — and she clearly couldn't tell good writing from bad. I was headed home and I'd find a treatment centre there that showed me more respect.

"You will give your First Step again next week — and I will make damn sure I'm here to hear it. This group is dismissed."

I sat there, leaning forward, head down, as if to protect myself from her next blow while everyone else got up to leave. No one came over to me to say thank you or to offer a hug. No one.

Dan at last stood up and lifted me by the arm. "Come on, let's go home."

I can't remember anything of the fifteen-minute walk back to our apartment. Dan had to leave after he got me inside, and I started making a sandwich. I was famished.

When the phone rang, I picked it up. It was another of my roommates. "How was your first step?" he said brightly.

"It was …" I broke down in sobs. I couldn't speak. My throat was so sore, I could barely breathe.

"Bob? Bob! What happened?"

"I … have … to … do it over."

"Really? I read what you showed me last night and it looked great to me."

"Well, it wasn't great to Nurse Ratched."

I hung up and just kept crying as I ate my sandwich, wondering what had just happened. I bounced between shame and resentment, landing on righteous vengeance to keep my spirits up and block the reality of what just occurred.

What did I do to deserve such a public humiliation? How did I screw up so hugely without a clue what I'd done wrong? Worst of all, how would I rewrite my First Step so I could "pass"? I didn't even know where to begin.

After lunch, I walked through the wooded path to an AA meeting being held in the same room as my disastrous performance that morning. In AA, as with other 12-step programs, whenever you speak, you first say your name, then follow that with "and I'm an alcoholic" — or in my case "an addict." This is because if you don't keep reminding yourself of that fact, it's easier to start denying it.

The therapist leading the group asked us all to check in, to quickly sum up how we were feeling. When my turn came, I said, "My name's Bob and I ... I ... I ..." then burst into tears. I couldn't talk.

I was acutely embarrassed at first, but then I wasn't and just let the tears flow. And flow they did. In fact, for the next three days, every time I said my name I would start to cry. I could never get past my name.

And this time, people didn't stay away. They came over and hugged me and held me and said, "Come here. Cry on my shoulder." And I did. Looking back on those three days, I see now that I was never alone. One morning, a therapist named Robin, whose name I knew but had never worked with, came up to me and asked me to come into his office.

After I sat down, he asked how I was doing.

"Not so good," I told him. "I can't seem to stop crying."

"That's good. You're getting better. Your treatment's ready to start."

I decided I couldn't just try to rewrite my first First Step and make it less self-serving and heroic. I had to start over with a blank page. I had realized it wasn't so much about hurting others, but about hurting myself. I got to work.

The next morning I gave my second First Step to everyone who'd heard my first one, Nurse Ratched included. When I was done, I still had it in a corner of my mind that if she failed me again, I would fly back to Toronto that afternoon and ... Well, I wasn't quite sure what I'd do.

When I finished, I again looked up and asked for feedback.

A woman raised her hand. "When you said you swore you wouldn't take coke after midnight, and then turned your clock back as it got closer to midnight, that reminded me of when I swore I'd stop forever — tomorrow morning."

When she finished, three more people raised their hands.

Then Nurse Ratched spoke. "Bob. I owe you an apology."

What did she just say?

"Obviously, you are a very good writer. Very seductive. But you use words to draw people in — all very charming — and then you use words to keep them at bay so that no one can really get close to you. I knew I had to attack your greatest strength in order to break down the astonishing denial you've built around your identity as a writer. Otherwise, you'd never get well. You'd leave and go out and use and likely die. I hear, though, that you're starting to get well. And now, you've passed your First Step. Good!"

I felt both relieved that I could now move forward in my treatment, and at the same time still a little cheated. If I hadn't screwed up my First Step the first time, I'd have been home sooner. Besides, I still felt ashamed of giving The Worst First Step in Talbott's History.

I waited for a few days after successfully completing my First Step before I called Jean. I wanted to make sure I wouldn't burst into tears on the phone. I know, she's the one person I should have been able to open up to. But it was way too soon for that, especially over the phone.

But I needed to speak to her, because with my First Step came a new privilege. After you'd been at Talbott for a month, your significant other was allowed a weekend visit. I likely exaggerated the strength of my relationship with Jean from the reality of us being very early in a relationship, into her being my long-time life partner when I argued my case that she be allowed to visit me. And they agreed, provided Jean attended an AA meeting with me on the Saturday morning after the two of us met with a couples' therapist at Talbott. They take the Ronald Reagan approach to patient relationships: trust but verify.

When Jean told the couples' therapist that she was a doctor who had been a psychiatric nurse, as if to assure her that she would be a trusted guardian for their patient for the rest of the weekend, the therapist looked straight at her. "Jean, what are you, a doctor, doing going out with a drug addict?"

"Well ... I only met Bob a few weeks ago, frankly, and we haven't really had a chance to establish our —"

"But it says here that you're his significant other."

Oh crap.

"Well, we were certainly going out with each other before he relapsed."

"You're a single mother, is that right?"

"Yes."

"Your children are all teenagers?"

"Yes."

"You know the chances of a relationship like this surviving are pretty slim, don't you, Jean?"

"Yes. Yes, I do."

"Good. Just so long as you know what you're getting into. Now both of you go to the AA meeting and then have a great weekend!"

And that was that.

All I can remember about the rest of Jean's first visit was a hotel room in downtown Atlanta where we enjoyed meals and sex and more meals and sex.

In the days after Jean left, I would call her every evening.

"Are you allowed to do this?" she would ask.

"Well, not every night."

"So, get off the line ... and call me tomorrow!"

I'd call the next night and give her a progress report — because I was making progress.

The next milestone for me at Talbott was Mirror Image, the eight-week internship at another treatment centre. This step was meant to allow patients to regain their self-respect and mirror their own addiction by working with other addicts.

Where you would be sent for your stint in Mirror Image was a mystery, determined solely by the therapists. You wouldn't dare ask where you thought you should be assigned, but we all discussed our preferred locations. I wanted to go to what I called the Rich-White-Folks psychiatric hospital, where I figured I could lead all the women in group therapy. I thought I'd be good at that. And there'd be no addicts around. Someplace toney would suit me just fine.

The day I got the call from Dr. Doug Talbott, the eponymous founder of the institution and a fearsome therapist, it was like getting a call from God.

"Tomorrow morning, we'd like you to start Mirror Image at Fulton County Detox," he said. "It's a one-week treatment ..."

I knew what it was. Fulton was located right in the middle of one of the worst crack neighbourhoods in America. The detox centre was free and funded entirely by the county. Nearly all its patients were young Black men and crack addicts, and it had a 95 percent failure rate — not surprising, given that the patients were in and out of there in a week. The dealers would wait across the street for them to leave to ensure they started using again.

Doug Talbott explained, "You're such a social being, Bob, that we want to take away all your social props so you can focus entirely on your addiction. You'll learn a lot." Then he hung up.

I can't survive there. I'll be killed.

I called Jean that night in a panic.

She heard me out, then said, "Just don't tell them you went to Princeton." I think she had a smile on her face as she hung up.

Maybe Fulton County was just what I needed.

Every weekday, three or four Talbott patients would pile into one of their cars and head to another treatment centre in the Atlanta area.

On that first morning, I arrived with my fellow Talbott patients outside what would be my workplace for the next eight weeks. All of them were doctors. Even though the owner of our car parked it on the street all day, he had no fear that someone would wreck it or steal it. Everyone in the neighbourhood knew that car had "the doctors from Talbott" who one day might save their lives inside Fulton County Detox. Our job was to be junior counsellors and to do physical and psychological intakes on incoming patients.

The staff at Fulton County just assumed I was a doctor and I didn't tell them I wasn't, nor did my Talbott friends bother with that tiny point, either.

This is how I ended up doing physical examinations on the new arrivals and leading group-therapy sessions throughout the day.

On the physicals, I learned to "bet the spread" between a patient's systolic pressure and diastolic pressure. Money was placed. Code words were uttered, and at the end of every week, one of us would have to buy the others lunch. We *were* addicts, after all.

Doing psychological intakes was a lot harder. I was the "second in" for a fellow Talbott patient, a forensic psychiatrist from Florida who was that rarest of all creatures: an aging white gay crack addict.

He taught me to always sit on the "door-side" of a meeting room in case the patient leapt across the table to attack me. He also taught me how to make the most of a bad situation.

"Look, these guys aren't going to open up to a couple of honkeys like us. They'll tell us nothing. So our job is to try to get through to them — fast — in even a tiny way. We need to make them *feel* what their smoking crack means."

He then told me we should craft a sentence that was guaranteed to get some kind of reaction. We came up with this: "Tell me, Tyrone. How did you feel when you stole that twenty-dollar bill from your mom's purse?"

We were sure they'd all done that, as had we. They worshipped their moms, as did we. It worked. A few started to cry. Most didn't react, except for their blush of shame. A few started to talk. One screamed at us.

Leading group-therapy sessions was tougher because I was on my own. How was I supposed to "lead" a dozen people in talking frankly about their problems when I'd never opened up about my own, had no training in how to help others do that, and not a single thing in common with them?

Except, of course, my addiction. Which I guess was Doug Talbott's point. Strip away all my social supports and defences. And put me face to face with the one thing we did all share, the one thing that brought us together — our addiction.

The first group session was a fiasco. I asked everyone to tell me their first names and what they "did." Big mistake. Only one or two "did" anything the way I meant it, and I was blind to the fact that I didn't "do" anything, either. So I changed my question to "What do you like to do?"

One woman, who called herself Lafayette Flowers, said she sang in a gospel choir.

I asked her if she'd like to sing something for us. I have no idea where that came from. My enthusiasm overrode my judgment. But sing she did, and she sang "Amazing Grace" beautifully.

It turns out lots of people in the group liked to sing, and this led to a little tradition: every time our group met, someone opened and closed the meeting by singing. And we all held hands as their voices filled the room.

That point was really hit home for me when I was one of two Talbott patients taking a group of Fulton County patients to an early evening meeting of Cocaine Anonymous.

We were driven there and back in a school bus, and our job was to make sure everyone checked in to the meeting, stayed there, and came back.

The meeting was in a church basement in downtown Atlanta. On the left as we walked in was a group of homeless men who were having dinner at a long table. On the right was the CA meeting. Since you could still smoke in public buildings back then, the entire room was dense with smoke.

Meetings here were not like the ones at Timothy Eaton Memorial in Toronto. The participants weren't soft-spoken and well-dressed. They weren't going to some fancy treatment centre like me. Cocaine Anonymous was the only thing that stood between them and jail or an early death. Their communities weren't like mine back home, made up of loving friends and fairly functional families. Theirs were often as desperate as they were.

After half an hour in the CA meeting, I couldn't take the heat and the smoke in the hall any longer. I told my colleague I was going to step outside for a few minutes. I went for a short walk and tried to process what all this meant. I still felt like a visitor to my own life, watching it instead of feeling it and living it. Yesterday I'd got a letter from my bank telling me they were repossessing my house. I wondered vaguely where I was going to live after I left Talbott.

But I pushed that unpleasant and very real thought away, as I'd always done, oblivious to the fact that this avoidance of reality was one reason I was here.

When I turned to go back into the church, a very large man was blocking the door. He glared at me.

"Hey," he shouted. "You an addict, or you homeless?"

It turned out he worked at the church and just wanted to direct me to the right meeting.

8 Family Week

Family Week at rehab is a scary time. The patients are still in denial about the damage their addictions have caused, and now their families arrive to say, in front of everyone, "You didn't dent the car. You *stole* a car and crashed it and almost *killed* the other driver," or some other truth.

One patient, an ophthalmologist from Florida, boasted to us for weeks how gorgeous his girlfriend was. He was right, but in one of our couples' sessions, when everyone began by "checking in," she turned to him and starting speaking, softly at first. "Mark, I'm so glad you're here. You need to be here. Please do what they tell you." Then her voice rose, her face reddening. "Last month after you left home to come here, I was cleaning out the bedroom and saw something on top of the closet. It was an old shoebox. There were a bunch of video-tapes inside. I took one out and popped it into the machine …" Here, she paused, her voice rising louder. "And I spent the next half-hour watching you having sex in our bed with different women."

He froze in his seat.

No one else in the room moved.

She glared at him, an avenging Valkyrie. "When I got here last night, I gave a copy to your therapist." She then lifted her big purse from the floor, opened it, and pulled out three more tapes. "And if anyone here wants to see them, just ask."

Hell hath no fury.

The term *Family Week* suggests you'll ask members of your family to come to the treatment centre to support you and learn some tools so they can help you stay clean and sober when you come home. Addiction is, after all, a family disease, and yes, my mother was an alcoholic.

But when I heard about Family Week, the thought of inviting either of my two half-brothers or my half-sister never entered my head. They were all much older than me and, although we weren't estranged exactly, we were not close. My parents were also long dead. As for my friends who'd intervened on me, I was so guilt-ridden that I felt I couldn't really ask them to step up.

But I felt I had to have someone attend (though not all the pa-tients did). I had to appear normal. I couldn't be alone, my loneli-ness exposed for all to see. Looking back, I doubt I gave any of my family or friends a second's thought and called Jean straightaway to ask her. I explained that it wasn't really for a week, but rather for three days. She said she'd call back the next day with her answer.

When she called back to say yes, I was desperately relieved.

Two weeks later, Jean arrived in Atlanta, checked in to the Comfort Inn nearby, and made her way to Talbott.

The first Family Week event was a Welcome Barbeque that first evening. I introduced Jean to my roommates and my therapy group mates and their families. It was a bit like a cocktail party back home, with everyone being very light and chatty. But the alums — those who'd been in treatment elsewhere — knew what was to come the next morning.

All of Talbott's eighty patients at that time lived in a low-rise apartment block within walking distance of the main building.

I had three roommates my first month: Ted, a defrocked priest who was an alcoholic and a sex addict; Gord, a kidney surgeon from Dallas who'd been one of the youngest colonels in the U.S. Air Force; and Dan, a doctor from Ottawa who was a fentanyl addict.

On our way back to Jean's hotel after the picnic, I asked her if she liked my friends.

"Well ..." she said slowly, "I don't think I've ever met such a smart, charming, articulate group of sociopaths in my life."

I guess she'd know, given her experience as a nurse at CAMH before she became a doctor.

The next morning, we were split into smaller family groups, and the spouses were asked to introduce themselves. By the time Jean's turn came, we'd heard all kinds of stories of spouses, generally wives, saying that this was not their first Family Week, by any means. By this stage, they were just trying to hold the family together, not lose the house, and keep the kids from checking out entirely, either by disengaging or by raging, in order to cope with the chaos at home. They'd heard their husbands' promises before, and while they hoped this time would be different, painful, family-demolishing experience told them it was unlikely.

"So, Jean, tell us about yourself," the therapist asked.

"Well, I'm a physician from Toronto and I ... I don't really know why I'm here. I don't know Bob that well ..."

What is she saying?! My heart sank.

"Do you live together?" the therapist asked.

Jean laughed. "No, no."

The fact is, our relationship was a huge secret — to Jean's medical colleagues and her friends of many years, and certainly to her ex-husband. And while her kids would occasionally see me when I stayed the night at their house, they knew nothing about me — and seemed to care less.

Over the next three days, Jean and I went to classes and groups and AA meetings together.

On the second day, just before the 8:00 p.m. AA meeting, Jean arrived outside the meeting hall.

"Bob, I can't stay here. I'm going to go home tomorrow."

"What?" Panic.

"I don't know what I'm doing here."

"No, no, you have to stay."

"No, really. I'm going to go back to the hotel, pack my bags, and take the first flight out tomorrow morning. You'll be fine without me."

"No!"

Why was she doing this? She couldn't leave me.

"Jean, what's wrong?"

At that moment, a female patient I was friends with walked by with her partner in tow. She was about sixty, an alcoholic, and a nurse. Jean had met them at the picnic. "Shall we go in?" she said.

"Jean doesn't want to," I said.

"What? Why not?"

We all turned to look at Jean.

"Because I don't know what I'm doing here. I've made a big mistake coming, and now I need to get back to my children."

It was clear by now that Jean had flown to Atlanta for her own reasons as well as mine. They had to do with her failed first marriage and the problems with her teenage kids. Being in what Talbott called "a safe place," and in an environment familiar to any former psychiatric nurse, had unpacked some of Jean's own issues — and she was only now becoming aware of them.

I was completely undone. Panic tied my tongue.

My friend said, "Sure, okay. But you're here now and we're all going in, so let's go to the meeting together."

We did, and for the next hour I tried desperately to think how I could keep her there. If she left the next morning, I was sure she'd never see me again. That she'd view me as just a fling, a wild, risky, crazy boomerang relationship after splitting from her husband the year before. That this whole thing, especially her coming here, was insane.

After the meeting, I had to go back to my room in order to make curfew, as did my friend. Her partner said she'd walk Jean back to the hotel where all the families were staying.

My last words to Jean were "Stay, honey. Please stay." I had never felt as desperate as I did at that moment.

All she said was "Goodnight."

These were pre-smartphone days and our outside calls from Talbott were very limited. So, when I woke up the next morning, I didn't know if Jean was at the hotel, at the airport, or in the air. When I called the hotel, I was told she hadn't checked out, but that she wasn't in her room.

At breakfast in Talbott's cafeteria, I saw my friend from the night before and waved her over. "Have you seen Jean?"

"No."

"I guess she's gone."

"Bob, I think you should let her tell you."

I'd pushed a boundary and got pushed back.

Despondent, I made my way from breakfast to our first class. What would I say to everyone? That we really weren't that close? Or worse, that she didn't like what she saw in our first day and decided to not waste another single day of her life waiting to end this no-hope relationship?

Five minutes into the class, the door opened and in walked Jean. She apologized for being late, said she had gone for a long walk and got lost on her way back.

I couldn't wait for the class to end.

When it did, I asked her what happened.

"Well, your nice friend took me back to the hotel and asked me for coffee. Pretty soon, there were other women from Family Week — half a dozen of them. We all crowded around the table. I told them I had to leave.

"We talked — in a way I'd never done in my life, even when I was counselling alcoholics. When the hotel closed the coffee shop for the night, we went upstairs and continued to talk in my room.

"We talked for three hours. Not just about me, but about all of us. They told me about their panic, their need to flee, their determination to stick it out.

"By the time we all went to bed, one thing was clear. My wanting to leave last night had nothing to do with you. It had everything to do with my failed marriage, and how I'd stuck it out long after it was over. Since I left him over a year ago, I'd never given myself the time to, as they say here, process it all. I cried and cried when we were talking, and those women held me and hugged me, it felt like all night long. They were wonderful."

"So, you'll stay?"

"I guess I need to," she said, a big smile on her face.

9 "I Don't Know If You've Got the Stamina ..."

A fter I'd returned from treatment to Toronto, I introduced Jean to my great friend and accountant, Arthur Gelgoot.

Arthur didn't act like an accountant, which attracted a large number of creative types to his practice — artists and writers who would come in at tax time with a garbage bag full of receipts and say, "Help me, Arthur!"

Arthur, along with my best friend Charles Fremes, was the one who had intervened on me, and he kept his eye on me when I got back from Atlanta.

It turned out Jean had needed Arthur's help, as well. In 1990 she was paying 18 percent interest on a mortgage, and, as he counselled her on her first visit, she was slowly going broke.

I went into his office two days before I had to file my 1990 return to talk with Arthur, whose staff had filled in my forms. With the April 30 tax deadline, Arthur's office was packed the entire month, but, as always with Arthur, you didn't small-talk for a couple of minutes then get down to business. You small-talked, listened to his latest CD, heard all the gossip for twenty-eight minutes, then finally got down to business in the last two minutes of your half-hour appointment. But those two minutes were magic. He made it all so clear.

If you had a problem with Revenue Canada, he'd say he'd call them the next day and clear it up. And not only would he call, he'd actually clear it up. On this visit, sometime during our first twenty-eight minutes, Arthur asked about Jean. We were about three months into our relationship at that point, and I said, "She's terrific. Things are going well."

Arthur replied, "I don't know, Bob. I'm not sure you've got the energy to keep up with Jean Marmoreo."

What? Is he kidding me?! I have the energy of ten men.

I didn't say anything. We talked taxes and I left his office. In the waiting room I saw Jean. "What are you doing here?"

"My taxes. And you?"

"Taxes."

"When are you going in?"

"Right now, I think."

I sat and waited the half-hour for her.

As we were taking the elevator down together, I asked her how it went.

"Much better than I thought," Jean said. "But Arthur did say he wasn't sure I had the energy to keep up with you."

10 The Thousand-Mile Hike

As a family physician, Jean spent her days in her family practice clinic giving people news, sometimes reassuring but often very bad. The tickle in the chest that ends up being lung cancer. The bad biopsy result. Committing a schizophrenic teen because they're harming themselves and their families. Some doctors are dreadful at this — often the older ones, who didn't have the benefit of "bedside manner" courses at med school, and, of course, in my experience, surgeons.

I'd heard about Jean's wonderful bedside manner from her patients, how she really listened to their concerns and was there for them. This was confirmed by her online ratings, which are usually a feeding ground for angry souls, but in her case seemed to be troll-free.

By the time I'd been living with Jean for a year, I'd learned to read the early signs that some news was coming: the biggest one was No Warning At All. Like when we were washing the dishes after dinner (a relatively new skill for me) one night in 1991 and she turned to me and said, "You know I'm turning fifty next year?"

"Sure."

"Well, I've decided I'm going to take three months off next summer, bring in a locum, and hike the Appalachian Trail."

Before I could even process the three actions in that sentence, she said, "If you want to join me, that's fine. But if you don't, I'll go on my own. I'm doing it for me."

It took me awhile to understand what "it" was. What the hell she was talking about?

"Really?" I said.

At least I didn't ask "What's the Appalachian Trail?"

Looking back, that indiscretion could have cost me my place on the trip, and thus our relationship and our lives as "ends-of-the-earth" explorers together. This was pre-internet days, so I couldn't just ask Siri "What's the Appalachian Trail?" It took until the next day and a call to the library, when I was told the AT was a hiking trail that ran along the top of the Appalachian Mountains from northern Georgia to Maine. While millions of Americans hiked small parts of it on weekends, its 2,100 miles took six months to hike from end to end. Of the two thousand "thru-hikers" who set out each April from Springer Mountain in Georgia to trek the entire trail by September, only five hundred would make it to Mount Katahdin in Maine.

I guessed if Jean wanted to take three months off, she wanted to hike "only" half the trail.

Well, that was a relief; kind of like only having to run half a marathon when you were expecting to run an entire one — with no training and not a clue what you were doing.

Was she crazy? What had prompted this ridiculous mission? And what about *me*?! I'd never been to summer camp, let alone spent ninety days trekking up and down the oldest mountains in North America with a heavy pack on my back. I wouldn't know a tent peg from a bear cub. True, I'd done an Outward Bound canoe trip in 1986, but that was for a week (during which I almost drowned), not twelve weeks. And we'd had guides; far from the idea of two city slickers out on our own in the wild.

But what if I didn't go with Jean? Cripes, I'd be alone with her kids, who were more likely to maul me than the bears on the trail. But much more important, I knew at some deep unspoken level, this was a test, if not *the* test. Jean was saying, "I've been here for you this past year since your rehab. You've been here for us. But if we're going to be with each other for good, I need to know you're *really* going to be here."

That was only the first of the items on that test. She'd taken me in (and taken a huge chance in doing so) after I left Talbott. She'd had faith in me when lots of people were turning away. She knew her already fractured family could be torn apart if I relapsed again. In so many ways, she'd given me back my life.

Looking back, I said yes to the trip for a jumble of reasons. Jean was easily the most adult woman I'd ever lived with. This made her alluring and frightening at the same time, since I had no experience with such creatures and, as with so much else in my life, I didn't know how to act around her. I didn't know the rules. But in this case, I lacked the confidence I could just make them up as I went along and hope to survive. I was also afraid that if I didn't go, our relationship would wither and die. This is a variation of the oldest trope in my life: I must say yes, because if I say no, they will disappear and leave me all alone. Or I flee. Either way, if I don't say yes, I end up alone.

Jean had also hung in as I'd continued to betray myself. That's the thing about addicts and alcoholics. We set up our friends and loved ones to be disappointed in us, and then we resent them when they back away. When they stay, it's hard not to push them away. Being freshly clean and sober, I had a whole lot of learning and relearning to do.

That said, I can't remember the exact moment I made the final decision to join Jean on the trek. But I suspect at the time I was still playing by the one rule that my friends in Alcoholics Anonymous made it easy to follow: Not "One day at a time," but "Shut up and get in the car."

Besides, the hike would be an adventure, and that was one addiction I'd never lose.

The next day I asked the senior partner in the communications firm I had landed in when I got back from Atlanta if I could take three months off the next summer. I told him the plan. He looked dubious but said yes. I was bringing in lots of new business, so he was betting I'd more than make up when I got back what he would be paying me while I was gone. Jean would have to pay for a locum, a part-time doctor, to fill in when she was away — and pay that doctor what she would have earned. Her financial sacrifice speaks to the need she felt to mark her fiftieth birthday — and change her life.

And so it was that in the spring of 1992, Jean and I were testing our gear and endurance on weekends at campgrounds north of Toronto.

Once, early on a Saturday evening, we knew we couldn't hike to our campground before dark, so we decided to pitch our tent in the corner of a farmer's field. We'd get up with the sun and be off and not bother anyone. But we slept in past sunrise, and when we woke, we looked out the front of our tents to see staring back at us a herd of buffalo. In Southern Ontario? Buffalo? It turned out we'd camped out on the only domestic buffalo farm east of the Prairies. Ten minutes later, the owner drove by and shooed us off his land. It was good that we looked old and inept — a skill we'd refine to great advantage on the AT.

During these weekend test hikes, we tried out our gear and got in shape for the much tougher days that lay ahead, when we'd be doing nine to twelve miles a day with our home, food, and clothing on our backs. While these practice runs got us in the mindset for the Trail, we learned that nothing prepares you for the real thing better than the thing itself — and that, in terms of gear and fitness, we were woefully unprepared for what lay ahead.

Taking three months off work requires other planning, as well. Jean did hire a locum to care for her patients when she was gone, but, of course, there were still the kids. We were going to leave them alone in the house all summer long. Jean's daughter Lara, the oldest at eighteen, was followed by Jean Paul, then sixteen, and MaryBeth (now Ryan), just twelve. We weren't worried they'd turn the house into a nightclub or a drug den, but knew they'd argue loudly over everything. We also knew they were closer to each other than to their friends, and certainly to us, or rather, to Jean. A year into living with them I was still on probation, still a bit of a resident stranger in the household. So, once the decision had been made, we sat the kids down and pledged to call them once a week from the Trail. We told them we'd met with our accountant to make sure the bills would all be paid and there would be enough money for them while we were gone. We told them we'd updated our wills. They just sat there and yawned.

Since Jean's fiftieth birthday was on August 30, and we'd be alone on the Trail, I thought we needed to celebrate this big occasion with a surprise birthday party in Toronto before we left. And not just any night, but the very night before we left. I enrolled Jean's kids in the planning, invited fifty friends, got home early to decorate the backyard, knowing Jean would arrive late from her clinic because she was always late and this night she'd be frantically so.

What was I thinking? Of course we hadn't packed or even bought all our gear. What we had done was send some food boxes ahead to the designated post offices in tiny Appalachian towns where we'd check in after coming off the Trail to restock.

When I saw Jean pull in to the driveway, I signalled for everyone to be quiet. As she walked in, the first person she saw was her sister, and her first thought was that her mother had died, thinking, *Joyce would never drive in from Dunnville unannounced unless ...*

But the party was wonderful and Jean put on a good face, though she was aware she still had hours of packing ahead of her and we had a very early plane to catch to Atlanta the next morning. Everyone had left by 10:00 p.m., and this is when the kids decided to sit Jean down to watch *Deliverance*. She'd never heard of the movie, so like good teenagers anywhere, they helped us celebrate what would presumably be our impending kidnapping by six-fingered, banjo-playing, southern crackers. Jean was not amused.

We flew to Atlanta early the next morning. It was raining torrentially when we landed. When we got to the bus station, we approached a cabbie and asked if he could take us to Springer Mountain, the location of the trailhead and the southernmost point of the Trail.

Even lifting our backpacks into the car took huge effort. How were we going to carry them on our backs for three months?

The cabbie could see that we weren't weekend hikers at all. "You're late," he said. "Thru-hikers come through in April. It's June. You won't make Maine before it starts to snow."

"We're only doing half," I said.

"Ah, okay. Get in."

We got to talking during the drive, and he told us he was an army veteran who'd served in North Dakota, where he did Arctic training. He was Black and very proud he'd risen in the ranks to become a sergeant. One of his sons was a Marine; another a police officer.

I asked early on if he knew where we could get fuel for our stove.

"Sure do," he replied. "Miss Emma's, about five miles from the mountain."

Our plan was to spend the first night at the hotel at the foot of the mountain, then set off the next day. That was looking like a life-saving prospect, as the heavy rain continued to fall.

Well into the two-hour drive north from Atlanta, while our cabbie was regaling us with war stories about his days in North Dakota, I asked what he did after he was discharged.

"Well," he replied slowly, "I wasn't exactly discharged. More like busted. I spent a year in the brig. When I got out, I worked as a truck driver, then bought this cab."

"Busted?" I asked faintly.

"Yeah, we'd all been drinkin' one night. Guy came at me, pulled a knife. MPs came later and found his finger in my pocket."

"He was trying to pick your pocket?"

"No, he was long gone. But I got his finger."

Silence filled the car as we absorbed this fact and realized our possibly perilous situation as he turned off the highway. "Where are we going?" I asked, reaching for the Swiss Army knife in my pocket.

"Miss Emma's. You wanted fuel, right? She's just up the road."

As we drove on, the road got narrower and darker with each mile, eventually becoming a dirt road, then a path. When the cab pulled to a stop outside a ramshackle cabin on the edge of a wood, I looked at Jean in an attempt to signal *Get your knife, stay in the car, and I'll be out in a flash. If I'm not, come and get me. If he takes off with you, stab him in the neck.* I'm not sure she got all that in the two seconds I looked at her, but I got out of the cab, walked gingerly to the front of the shack, and yelled, "Miss Emma? Miss Emma!"

"Right here, boy. Wud you want?"

In the darkness, an older woman sat behind a counter. There was nothing on the shelves. I stepped inside. "The taxi driver said you could sell me some white fuel for our camp stove."

"White fuel?"

"Yes, camping fuel."

"How much you want?"

"A quart? Anything, really. We're headed out on the Trail tomorrow."

"Oh, I know that, boy."

She got up, went to a backroom, re-emerging a few seconds later with a quart-sized tin. She showed me the top and let me smell it. It was just what we needed.

"How much is that?" I asked.

"Two dollars."

"Two dollars?"

"That too much for you?"

"No, no, it's fine. It's perfect."

I peeled off two crumpled dollar bills, turned, and almost ran back to the cab, a huge grin on my face. They could still kill us both, but the odds were shrinking.

"How far to Springer Mountain?" I asked as I got in the cab.

"Five miles," said the cabbie.

Ten minutes later, we drove up a steep hill to a country inn. The rain stopped when we did. We paid the driver, including a big tip for not killing us, we all wished each other well, and went inside to check in.

That night, we had a lovely dinner in the dining room, both knowing the real test would begin tomorrow. Neither of us was up to that test, but neither of us was going to confess that across the candlelit table, either.

If the first week on the Trail was utter hell, the first hour was the hot lick of its flames. There's a great scene in the movie *Wild*, where the hero, Cheryl Strayed, played by Reese Witherspoon, is in her messy motel room the night before she sets off on what seems a suicidal hike from Mexico to Washington State along the Pacific Crest Trail. She has all her gear spread out on her bed, on the floor, on the toilet seat, everywhere. She's soon stuffing everything into her very large pack. In the next scene, she's lying on her back with the pack under her, struggling to heave both herself and it off the floor — a turtle flailing on its back.

That was us. We'd failed to actually weigh our packs before strapping them onto our backs. What was meant to be forty pounds each had swelled to fifty, and our aching muscles and bleary spirits screamed at us daily. Your enjoyment of the Trail is inversely proportional to the weight of the pack.

We set off on a typical June day in Georgia, with clear skies and temperatures of ninety degrees Fahrenheit. We took pictures at the trailhead, which was just a hole in the woods. Here, we learned our first lesson in trail-hiking: trailheads are always at the lowest point of any trail, so the first hour of trekking involves a steep upward climb.

So where were we sixty minutes into our three-month journey? Creaking under the weight of our packs and thirsty from the heat, gulping down our precious water supply at a feverish pace.

I wanted to go home.

But I was damned if I was going to quit in front of this woman who had dragged me back to Georgia, which I'd last visited as a patient in rehab. Jean always seemed so much stronger than me. She just put her head down, put one foot in front of the other, and made her way up the mountain.

Just fifteen minutes in, I called out, "I have to rest."

Jean looked back at me. "Okay."

I took off my pack, drank some more water, caught my breath, then started up again.

Fifteen minutes later: "I have to rest."

"Okay."

And so it went until we reached the first peak at noon that first day. It wasn't a peak, really, because that implies a pointy top, like Everest; it was simply a high point on a rolling mountain that had so many trees on top we couldn't see more than a hundred feet in any direction. So much for glorious mountain views. We took off our packs and ate our sandwiches in silence.

"How you feeling?" I finally asked Jean.

"Well, it's a slog. You?"

"I'm not sure I can do ninety days of this." In all honesty, I knew I couldn't do ninety more minutes.

"Stay in the moment, dear. Don't catastrophize."

Ah yes, lessons from AA — *One day at a time.*

I think what saved me is that I was too tired to even talk. This kept me from saying what every particle of my body screamed to say: *I quit!*

A week later, Jean confessed that she, too, had wanted to pack it in, in that first hour. But she was damned if she'd quit in front of me.

You may ask, where do you sleep on the Trail?

Generally, in a shelter: a three-walled stone structure that holds twelve to sixteen hikers. The fourth side is comprised of a chain-link fence with a small opening that's shut at night to keep the bears out and you safely in.

All your food needs to be hoisted up via a big pole until it is very high up a tree trunk outside, again, to keep it from the bears. The only animals inside the shelter are the mice, who love to gnaw through your boots and, of course, your head pack, where you keep your stash of midnight snacks. I woke up one morning to find a two-inch hole chewed into my head pack, with a bunch of raisins neatly piled on the plank beneath my sleeping bag. The mice had eaten all of the nuts but had turned up their noses at the raisins.

Along the Trail, there's a shelter about every nine miles, but you can't book your space: it's first come, first served. So, what happens if too many hikers turn up? The late arrivals have to sleep outside in their tents, with their food bags also hoisted very high indeed, away from the bears.

The Appalachian Mountains are old, so their peaks are beaten down, but there are lots of valleys and even more gaps where rivers flow and the occasional road runs through. The first gap we got to was Neels Gap, thirty miles and four gruelling days north of the trailhead, near the tiny town of Three Forks, Georgia.

Neels Gap is something to write home about only because it has a post office. It's there that exhausted hikers first off-load their excess gear — the shovel you thought you needed to bury your toilet paper with, the extra sweater (in this heat?!), the hardcover book, the axe.

These items and more like them were sitting in a box outside the Neels Gap Post Office for anyone to pick up and make their own.

Inside the post office we found something even better: one of the five food boxes we'd mailed ahead weeks before leaving home. We tore it open like eager mice, finding the dried eggs, instant coffee, pasta, and porridge we'd packed.

It came as a big surprise, after just four days on the trail, how much we were eating. We thought each box of food would last us two weeks, but it turned out to be more like ten days. We knew there were small towns you could hike to just off the Trail for the entire length up to Maine. And since pack-weight was always the biggest worry, the idea of stocking up in these towns (and maybe resting for half a day and eating a restaurant meal) soon became our obsession. So, a few days up the Trail, we decided to do something we'd never dared even think of doing before leaving home: we decided to come off the Trail and hitchhike to the nearest town. That's right. Get a lift from a total stranger … in deepest Georgia.

You're out of your minds! Have you not seen Deliverance*!?*

Despite this passing thought, I stuck out my thumb on the shoulder of a small road leading to the town, five miles away. Amazingly, the first car that drove by stopped and backed up.

The driver opened the window. "Where you headed?"

He sat in a semi with a Confederate flag in the back window and a rifle in the sling behind.

Oh god, what are we doing?!

He didn't look like the type who'd kidnap us. Or did he?

"Going to Franklin?" I inquired.

"Yup, hop in."

Jean and I piled in the back seat.

"Where you folks from?"

"Canada. You?"

"Couple miles back. Thru-hikers?"

"Yes."

"You two hitchhike a lot back home?"

"No. No, we don't."

"I don't pick up hitchhikers, either … This is my first time."

"Really? Same here."

"Wow."

There followed a collective exhalation of breath.

He was a high school teacher and was struck by our diminutive size and the giant packs we were carrying. If this was pity, so be it.

Each of us confessed that we were terrified the other was going to kill us. He said he kept a pistol in the door of his semi, just a quick draw away. All I had was my Swiss Army knife.

A short while later, we said goodbye to the kind stranger who, like the cabbie who drove us to the trailhead, came to represent the

"Trail Magic" — chunks of great good luck (and truly good people) — that befell us all along the route.

After a few weeks on the Trail, Jean and I had become veteran hikers. Peaks and distances that once exhausted us were now within reach. I no longer needed to stop every fifteen minutes to catch my breath.

My pack, which weighed fifty pounds when we arrived at the first post office at Neels Gap, weighed forty pounds when we left and pretty much stayed there for rest of the journey.

We got into a rhythm, making and breaking camp faster each day. An unspoken division of duties guided us to ever more efficient living: when we got to the shelter area each night, we'd both pitch the tent and blow up the air mattresses, I'd find the nearest creek to pump fresh water for cooking and drinking, and Jean would cook. In fact, she became a gourmet trail chef, creating new dishes from canned tuna and freeze-dried chicken. One-pouch meals were for *them*, not *us*.

We also became veteran hitchhikers, coming off the Trail every seven days. We learned to put our packs up high on our backs to make them look even bigger. We learned to say three vital words within the first minute of getting in the back seat of a car: *Canadians*, *doctor*, and *writer*. We wanted to appear as harmless as possible.

Our drivers were fascinated to learn how we ended up on the Trail. We'd always ask if they were hikers, too, and not once did we come across any who had actually hiked, let alone for ninety consecutive days. Another surprise was how they reacted to the fact that Jean was a Canadian doctor. Remember, we were in Appalachia, the poorest, sickliest, most inward-looking part of America. And what did we hear? "Socialized medicine, huh?"

This was 1992. There was no internet. No reason at all to even think about the Canadian health-care system, and yet this was their first reaction. Had these Appalachians been over-schooled in the evils of communism and its nicer cousin? Or did they subscribe to *Foreign Affairs* and not tell anyone? It was a mystery how the idea of socialized medicine ever found its way to the Appalachians, but it kept the conversation going for miles.

We also learned to love the tiny towns we ended up in. First stop, the laundromat, where we'd off-load our truly stinky clothes for a double-wash. Then down the main street to a Denny's or KFC, where we'd order a bucket or even a barrel — and believe me, we'd eat it all.

We were now hiking ten miles a day on the trail (far more than those first pitiful weeks). Jean figured we were burning 7,500 calories each day. Really? Well, a marathoner burns 2,600 calories for about four hours of running. But we were hiking for ten hours a day and carrying forty-pound backpacks up and down mountains. So, it didn't really matter how much we ate. Eight pieces of fried chicken? Done and gone.

If we got into a town late in the day, we'd also check in to the Bide-a-Wee Motel, where the rooms cost twenty bucks a night. We'd bask in the shower and clean our aching bodies, then tumble into their rundown beds that felt to us like the Four Seasons. Even the worst shower was better than the best cold river, for washing both our clothes and ourselves. The next morning it would be thumbs out on the highway, then back on the trail, always heading north.

Risk didn't just lurk everywhere on the Trail that summer — broken legs, rattlesnakes, Lyme disease, bad water — it talked to us constantly. This wasn't anxiety-inducing. We just got used to it, as people do when they do pretty much the same things every day for three months.

In fact, it was liberating. I felt oddly free for the first time in my life. How did I escape addiction and land upright in the arms of this marvellous woman who was older, fitter, faster, and went farther than I ever could?

The sign-in books at the shelters were filled with notes of gratitude from recovering alcoholics, how nature and the Trail were reconnecting them to the world again. For me, the biggest danger was forgetting to be grateful and thinking my addiction was an aberration brought on by … well, my addiction.

There were other dangers.

By July, we'd hiked through Georgia and North Carolina. One of our first nights in Virginia, we camped where the Trail crossed the Blue Ridge Parkway, which links Shenandoah National Park with Great Smoky Mountains National Park some 470 miles away. It's one of America's great scenic drives, along the crest of the Blue Ridge Mountains with stunning views of the valleys spread out below.

We'd heard all the stories about hikers being kidnapped or murdered in their sleep by crazy mountain men who knew every nook and cranny of these woods. We learned that the farther away from a road you were and the higher you hiked, the less likely a serial killer (who one assumes is not in great shape) will climb to do you in.

But we were tired that night, and it was getting dark, so we pitched our bright red tent on a grassy knoll some fifty yards from the parkway, where we could see the glow of headlights from the very few cars that travelled this stretch of road. As we had every night on the trail, we fell asleep the minute our heads hit the rolled-up shirts that doubled as pillows.

We were jolted awake around midnight by the sound of a motorcycle travelling along the parkway below. We could see its headlights growing larger against our tent. Suddenly, the sound of the engine stopped, though the light continued to illuminate our tent. I took a quick peek out the front flap. A hundred yards away was a guy dressed in leathers resting on what looked to be his Harley. While his light was on our tent, he was looking elsewhere, a cigarette in his mouth. Then he leaned over his bike and turned out the light.

Who was he? Why did he pull up in the middle of nowhere in the middle of the night? Flat tire? Should we get up and offer to help?

Then in the distance I saw the headlights of a car approaching from the other way. As it got closer, its lights also played across our tent. The driver must be able see it. The car slowed and turned suddenly, coming to a stop next to the motorcycle.

Oh shit. They knew each other. We could hear their voices but not their words. I'd learned some valuable street skills while in Fulton County Detox in Atlanta.

This could only be one thing: a drug deal. And we were right in the middle of it. Somehow, I knew their weapons would be more deadly than my Swiss Army knife. Why hadn't we pitched our tent higher and not out in the open where anyone could see us — and perhaps kill us to eliminate any witnesses?

Jean and I didn't speak, mainly because our hearts were in our throats. The two men talked for no more than a minute. We heard the sound of car doors opening and closing. Then the bike revved to a start and took off the same way it came. Same with the car, its tail lights growing faint as it disappeared behind a mountain. Finally, there was only silence and darkness.

Trail Magic strikes again.

We ran into the opposite of Trail Magic, as well. Mountains are risky places, especially on bright sunny days when you think there's nothing to fear.

One day we dropped down off the trail into the Nantahala Gorge in North Carolina and came to a river with a café beside it. We found out we could rent river rafts to paddle down the river, whose whitewater churned under a nearby bridge.

We hopped aboard an old school bus that took us five miles upstream where we got into a small rubber ducky of a raft. The day was sunny and hot, easily over ninety Fahrenheit. The river was calm and we gently paddled our way downstream back toward the café.

Then, half a mile from our destination, the river turned from a quiet stream into a raging torrent. Then … bam! We were overboard, with our boat floating quickly away. We'd avoided a rock that lay dead ahead, but in steering around it we'd gone straight into a steep fall, hitting a submerged rock, which flipped us into the chilly water.

We'd both paddled in whitewater before, so we knew the first rules of survival: if your raft flips and you end up in the river, always face forward with your feet up, and always stay with your raft.

I came up for air facing backward with my feet dragging low and tried in vain to turn around. When I finally did and was able to see what rocks to avoid, an undertow whisked away my sandals. Gone. Now in bare feet, I scrambled to catch the ducky, which was floating quickly off to the bank of the river. I yelled to Jean, who was swimming for the shore, to stop and catch the raft. She did. I swam hard to get to where she was and we both beached on the grass a hundred yards from the café.

At least we were on land, and we had our raft, though not our paddles or my shoes. We carefully walked the raft to the end of the course and turned it in to the young man who'd seen us capsize and came out to rescue us. We were cold and embarrassed, limping to the café like a couple of drowned rats. Jean looked pale and she seemed to be shivering in her wet T-shirt.

I got my wallet out of the locker. "Honey, why don't I get you some hot chocolate?"

All she said was "Okay."

I told her to sit down on the deck outside in the sun and warm up.

When I brought her the cup of hot chocolate, she put it to her lips but could hardly drink. Her lips were blue. We sat there for five minutes with her barely uttering a word.

A woman came over to our table and spoke to Jean. "Hi, you seem to be cold. Why don't you let me take you to the ladies' room and we'll dry you off and put some warm clothes on?"

Ten minutes later, they emerged, with Jean now wearing a sweatshirt, sweatpants, and a hat. Her lips were no longer blue. The woman turned to me. "I'm a nurse. I could see she was hypothermic. You need to watch for that on the rivers here."

I was stunned and grateful. Getting hypothermia when the sun's boiling down on you? A tricky place, this Trail. But for the first time in our two years together, I saw Jean not as invincible, but as vulnerable. It took time to realize that her courage and determination could get her into trouble, blinding her to risk.

Actually, that blindness had already appeared one day after just a couple of weeks on the Trail.

It was another perfect day in the mountains. We were headed to a mountaintop in Virginia and wanted to stop for lunch at the overlook at the top.

We'd learned to spot snakes lying ahead on our path. They looked like thick sticks. Since the trail was only wide enough for one person, big snakes tended to lie across the entire path. The serpents were more commonly spotted in higher elevations, where they could catch some sun, rather than in the dark forests below. When we came across one, we'd carefully walk around it and be on our way.

That day, twenty yards ahead of us on the trail to the overlook, a large snake lay basking in the sun. We knew by his tail that this was a rattler, and he was huge. We quickly realized we couldn't go around him because the ground on both sides of the trail was covered with stinging nettles that had grown to six feet in height. The plant's name tells you everything you need to know: just touch the nettles gently and you'll be screaming in pain. You'll never want to touch a stinging nettle twice.

This presented a problem. We couldn't go over the rattler, or around him. And if he was basking in the sun, no doubt his friends and relations might be hidden amongst the stinging nettles.

So, we'll just rest here for a bit, maybe have our lunch and wait for the rattler to move on? I thought. But Jean was determined. Our goal was the top of the mountain. By noon. For lunch. And that's what we were going to do.

Snakes have no ears, so they don't actually hear noise; instead, they react to vibrations on the ground. So, when a snake was taking too long to move on, we would pick up some small stones from the trail and throw them to the side of where he was, hoping that he'd not like that — and move.

We tried this with the big rattler blocking our path.

Nothing.

But Jean refused to give up. She picked up a rock bigger than her hand and threw it way *way* up, hoping it would make a loud thud when it landed. It did. But the rock didn't hit the ground; it hit the snake.

That got his attention. He suddenly rose up in a coil, facing us, his tail rattling. He was mad.

"Jean. Jean! Just walk back slowly. Don't turn around. Don't run. I'm right behind you. Just unhitch your pack and keep walking backward." This is advice you give when you encounter a bear, not a snake. But I had to say something.

After a minute the snake put his head back down. He was still mad and continued his rattling, but he didn't come after us. He also didn't move.

Jean was madder still, and her defiance kicked in. "I'll be damned if a snake is going to keep me from having lunch."

I wasn't sure I agreed.

I did convince her to take off her pack and join me in eating a power bar while we assessed our situation.

"Okay," she said, heaving her pack up onto her back. "Let's roll down our sleeves, put on our gloves and toques, and walk through the stinging nettles around him."

Which we did. But during that ten-minute bushwhack through a field of poisonous plants where we couldn't see a foot ahead of us, my paranoia ran wild: our snake had signalled his fellow snakes, which were slithering below our feet, to attack us without mercy. He may even have sent pictures of us out to them just so they didn't bite the wrong hikers.

We eventually made it back to the trail safely. We even made it to the mountaintop beyond for a wonderful lunch with views for miles. And most of all, I got a real sense of just how willful the woman I was hiking with could be.

By the time we reached Harpers Ferry, West Virginia, due west from Washington, D.C., we'd hiked eight hundred miles. It had taken us eight weeks. Our muscles ached all the time. Our feet were blistered, our faces burned. We fell asleep the second our heads hit our sleeping bags.

But we'd never felt so alive or united. We weren't two people thru-hiking the Appalachian Trail; we were one. I lost twenty pounds and we were both in astounding shape. We'd learned to break camp with lightning speed. We each had our tasks, which we performed without a word. We endured torrential rainstorms knowing that the worst that would happen was we'd get a ten-hour soaking. Our boots would fill with water. Our protein bars would come apart in our hands. But we'd dry off when we reached the shelter and the sun would eventually come out.

We learned how to endure.

The Appalachian Trail headquarters is in Harpers Ferry, the symbolic halfway point of the Trail, at the top of a very long, steep hill. We got into town late in the afternoon and had just fifteen minutes to make it to the Appalachian Trail gift shop where we could buy our precious AT badges to sew on our backpacks. So, with forty-pound packs on our backs, we ran up that hill and made it on time and barely out of breath.

The next day we took the train into Washington, D.C., rented a car, and drove up to Connecticut, where we got back on the Trail.

Two weeks later, on our final day on the Trail, we came off into a tiny town called Tyringham, Massachusetts. There was a lovely B & B we thought we'd spend the night in, but when we arrived a big sign on the lawn read "No Thru-Hikers." This wasn't a discrimination issue; it was a public health issue. We stank to high heaven and the B & B didn't want us smelling up the place.

So, because that was the only place in town to stay, we headed back out on the Trail. By the time we came to the shelter, darkness had fallen. Because it was our final night and the nearest creek was half a mile away, we decided I wouldn't pump the water using our water filter; I'd just pop in a couple of iodine pills to kills the germs.

We gave ourselves a break.

But exactly a week after getting back home, Jean and I were struck with the cramps and vomiting of giardiasis, also known as "beaver fever," which had made its way through our systems from drinking that not-quite-disinfected water that final night.

Another lesson from the Trail: when they say "pump all your drinking water," they mean *all*.

When we got back home and for months afterward, people would ask us: "What was it like?" What was the most amazing … dangerous … glorious … whatever … thing that happened?"

I would trot out the rattlesnake story, or the hitchhiking tales, or even the time we slept under the fire trucks in the Waynesboro, Virginia, fire hall.

But Jean only ever told one story:

"It was late in the afternoon and I was coming down off the mountain very slowly. Bob was ahead of me and turned around to ask what's the matter. I told him I just needed to stop for a few minutes because I had a bladder infection. He took my hand and guided me down the last one hundred yards, then took my pack and set it and me down by a tree."

"He opened his water bottle. 'Here, take this. Let's make camp here.'

"He then took the water pump and the bottles to the nearest stream and started pumping enough water to make some tea. He came back, lit the stove and ... and as I looked at him doing all this, I realized that I'd always taken care of myself. I'd spent the last three years looking after my kids. Now I'd gotten involved with this completely inappropriate, high-risk guy, and here he was taking care of me."

Whenever Jean tells that story, I beam with pride. But over a quarter of a century after it happened, I still don't get it. I didn't rescue her from a deep crevasse; I just pumped some water to make tea. I guess it means that reliability and doggedness are the real scorecards in relationships and in life. At least they are in ours.

By the time we ended our time on the Trail together, it had taken two pretty unhappy people and turned us into a functioning couple. I can't remember a single time when we talked about our relationship or discussed what gives us pain and joy. Indirectly, of course and in a thousand ways. Directly, no.

Today, it's much the same. We just get on with life, fairly sure that our signalling system, the code we forged tramping up and down the Appalachian Mountains, will keep us close and guide us through what's now, as well as what's next.

We landed back in Toronto just before Labour Day. My sense was the kids felt we were interlopers, which is only natural when you're a teenager who's had the run of the house all summer. What forbidden things did they get up to that will remain family secrets forever?

Leaving three teenagers to fend for themselves for three months taught us an important lesson. It took two weeks to find a pay phone (there were no mobiles back then) in a small town off the trail in North Carolina. On that first call, Lara told us the tires on the car were all worn down, almost bald, and needed to be replaced. "Replace them, of course," Jean said. It would cost a thousand dollars.

We called a week later from another town farther north. Lara took her responsibilities as the oldest child seriously.

On this call, she said the electric bill was way higher than she thought it should be and we hadn't left enough money to pay it off.

To which Jean said, "Just pay the minimum and Bob will sort it out when we're back.

"But, Mom, it's *wayyyyy* high. What if they cut off our power?"

"Don't worry, dear. They won't do that."

Our next weekly call was from Franklin, North Carolina, one of hundreds of towns in the American south that had been euthanized by the freeway and the malls. I remember that call because this time I was on the line with Jean Paul when he said, "How much will it cost to fix the porch?"

"About a thousand dollars, I think."

I walked back to the country-store porch where Jean was resting, boots off, in a rocking chair. I told her the story. We talked it over, and I called our accountant to give Jean Paul the money. We never called home again.

At dinner with the kids our first night back, Lara was clearly still rattled by the electricity bill. "Did you pay the minimum?" Jean asked.

"I couldn't. It was over my Visa limit."

"Well, don't worry. Bob will go through all the bills with you after dinner."

Later, in the living room, I asked Lara to show me the bill that was worrying her so much.

On the top was the Toronto Hydro logo with our address below, and at the bottom was … well, I looked at the number, my eyes widening: "Total: $45,000." Which was three months at $15,000 a month.

There must be some mistake. "Lara, this is wrong. They've confused us with a big company. Did you call them?"

"No, Mom said to wait until you got home."

"Okay," I said slowly. "Let me call Hydro and get this cleared up."

I'd realized that, for much of the summer, Lara had been thinking our power would be cut off, and that we were both a couple of deadbeats.

Others waded in on a different issue.

It was only after we got back that a family lawyer-friend told us that it was illegal to leave a child under the age of sixteen to fend for themselves in a home where the parents are absent.

Really?

Really.

11   Just Married

The biggest lesson the Appalachian Trail taught Jean and me was that we were better together than apart. We were both badly wounded when we met and came into our relationship with our elbows up. This may sound odd, given that Jean and I are both people persons, with a large group of friends. In Jean's case, also with patients who not only respected her, they claimed to love her. When she announced she was retiring this past December after forty-six years as a family physician, she got emails from her patients saying, "If you quit, I will die." A tad extreme perhaps. But dozens and dozens of them wrote to her, citing her skill and compassion and her presence in even the worst situations. As one patient wrote on Jean's retirement website: "Her speech is wise, and the law of kindness is on her lips."

But when it comes to the trust needed to make a permanent and intimate relationship thrive, life had taught us to be guarded. We both hid our fears under waves of enthusiasm from me and kindness from Jean. But the fact was, we both approached life with our elbows up, letting people in with seeming ease. But only so far. Then, from whatever deep-seated fear of being hurt, we kept them at bay. For me, drugs was my tool of choice. For Jean, it was "hiding out in the delivery suite."

By the fall of 1992, I'd been out of treatment for well over a year. I was back on my feet at work and financially. I'd joined a small communications firm whose structure enabled me to rebuild some back into my own work and life. My relationship with Jean's kids would go sideways sometimes, and I had to temper my desire to have them trust and love me — totally and right now! — with the reality that, as Lara said once, "Mom, you've taken us away from Dad and moved us in with a drug addict — and you're a doctor!"

I was profoundly different from their father, who was tall, dark, Italian, and rarely spoke. Jean Paul came home after school one day and took out a copy of *The Old Man and the Sea* from his backpack. He sat down on the kitchen counter to read it. I said, "Oh, you're reading Hemingway. Isn't the young boy in it great?" Jean Paul stared up at me with a look of bewilderment and disgust. Then he went back to his page. *Hmm ... I guess he's not that into books.*

I tried again. "Do you think he'll catch the marlin?"

This time, I didn't even get a dark look. He stared harder at his page, hoping I'd just shut up and leave. *Has no one ever talked about books to this kid?*

It took a while to get used to the emotional protocols of this family I was now a part of. As with all families, the really important stuff rarely gets aired and shrivels up from lack of use. On the other hand, there were things — hidden, forbidden things — that Jean talked about as if they were the weather.

One day I came home early from work. I opened the door to our living room and there on the phone was Jean. Sitting on the stairs were Jean Paul and a girl I'd never seen before. Their faces were red and they looked like they wanted to be anywhere else but where they were.

"Hello, Mrs. Martin," I heard Jean say, "This is Jean Marmoreo, Jean Paul's mom. I got home a few minutes ago and met your daughter Allison, and it's very clear to me that she and Jean Paul will be wanting to have sex soon. So, if Allison has protection, that's fine. But if she doesn't, I'm happy to provide her with it. I just want to ask what you think."

At this point, I was one with Jean Paul. Not only would no one ever speak this way in my family, it was inconceivable they'd even think this way. Jean didn't seem upset. She saw this rite of passage as a purely clinical transaction. As with so much in her work and life, her view was that silence and screaming will get you nowhere, but talking can help.

I was in awe.

In the winter of 1992–93, we spent a week at a spa in Mexico. It wasn't a massage-and-hot-tub place, but rather one of healing modalities and cleansing diets. Not my thing. One night, all fifty guests stayed up late to form a circle around the campfire and sing and dance under the full moon. The next morning, I asked a large Swiss woman, who was on the staff, what she did back home. "Energy," she said over the breakfast table. To which I replied, "Oh? Electrical or nuclear?" She picked up her granola and left.

But it was on that holiday that Jean and I were out for a hike on a dusty mountain road near the spa. There was a rusty old can that I kicked forward. We'd walk a bit more, then Jean would kick the can. Then I'd kick it. Then it was her turn, and so on, and on we walked for a good mile, with each of us taking turns kicking the battered can a few steps. It would never go straight but slice off to one side or the other. In this way, it perfectly mirrored the conversation we'd started.

"So, we're living together and ..."

"What do you think about ..."

"About ..."

"Well, sure. I guess ... Maybe ... Yes ... If you want ..."

We kept this up for twenty minutes with no clear resolution whether we would or wouldn't. But the secret code of our deeply guarded linguistic probes was transmitted loud and clear.

Back home later that week, I got my mother's wedding rings out of my safety deposit box at the bank and waited for my chance. My mother had gotten married in 1948 and I only found out years later that they were her mother's wedding rings, as well.

Since my mom was forty-one when I was born in 1949 (daringly old to have a baby then), these rings had been working full-time from the early days of the twentieth century and, with any luck, would still be at work as we touch the third decade of the twenty-first.

All I cared about, though, was finding a time and place to propose. Our home was a rented four-bedroom house that had just one bathroom, so it was the busiest room in the place. Jean had been out for an evening run and was in the shower. I don't know why I thought that proposing to her while she was in the shower and I was outside the shower was romantic, let alone practical. But I did. While the shower was running full blast, I almost yelled, "Will you marry me?"

"What?!" Jean said from the other side of the curtain.

"Will you marry me?!"

"I can't hear you!"

I opened up the curtain and with the engagement ring held tightly in my hand, I asked for a third time, "Will you marry me?!"

Jean stood there, naked, with shampoo covering her head and face.

"What's this? What's in your hand?" She could barely see.

"A ring."

"A ring? Why?"

"Because ... it's an engagement ring ... I want you to ..."

She at last understood. "Oh, my heavens! Oh yes, yes, of course I will!" She reached for the ring and ... it dropped in the bathtub, heading straight toward the drain. She pounced and caught it just in time. I tremble to think.

And at that very minute, Jean's eldest daughter, Lara, burst into the bathroom. "What's all the yelling?"

"Oh honey," said Jean, still covered in soap and holding her ring tightly. "We're getting married!"

"I figured that was it," said Lara. "Let me see the ring."

"Let me get dressed, dear. I'll show it to all of you downstairs."

Our wedding was set for Sunday, July 25, 1993.

We were married in St. Mark's Anglican Church in Port Hope, across the street from our great friends David and Anita Blackwood, who hosted the reception in their large garden.

Months before, we had visited the Reverend Mary Redner at St. Mark's to tell her we wanted to be married in her church. I had gone to high school just up the road at Trinity College School, and we students had attended chapel once a day and twice on Sundays. In my senior year, I'd been the head choirboy.

We laid all this out for Mary and were taken aback when she said she'd be happy to marry us, but that she strongly recommended we take the Anglican Marriage Course beforehand.

We later learned this had nothing to do with my suitability for marriage, but Jean's. She'd been divorced, and she was a Presbyterian. I didn't bother telling Mary I was a drug addict, but she seemed to be thrilled that I had been the head choirboy.

So off we went one Saturday morning to an Anglican Church in Toronto for our weekend course in marriage. There were thirty other couples in the pews when we arrived, all far younger than us. We held our noses very high. What were we doing here? These were kids! Life hadn't happened to them yet.

The course leader was a retired Anglican minister. He got right to the point by asking a young couple in the front pew to come up to the altar. He asked them all the usual welcoming questions, then turned to the woman and said, "And what if he yells at you?"

She seemed confused.

He asked again. "What if he yells at you? What will you do?"

"Uh ... yell back?" She seemed to be trying to find the right answer and began floundering. "Well, I'm not sure ..."

"Okay, what if he hits you?"

She turned red. Her fiancé frowned.

This was getting interesting.

"Hit me? I'd leave."

"You'd leave, is that right?"

"Yes, of course." She was very sure now. "I'd walk out."

"So ..." the course leader said, turning to all of us, "how many of you would leave if your spouse hit you?"

Every hand went up.

"That's good," he said. "But sadly ... it's not true."

Much rustling in the pews.

"The fact is, it takes an average of six beatings before a woman will leave her abusive husband. Not one. Six. And this weekend, we're going to dig into why that is and why half of you will not be married to your fiancé ten years from now."

"Welcome," he said with a very large smile, "to the Anglican Marriage Course."

We were riveted.

At noon, we were on our own for lunch, so Jean and I walked

over to a nearby strip mall to find a coffee shop. We went in and there he was, the course leader, sitting alone eating a sandwich. He welcomed us over and we sat down. Over lunch he told us that the course was created at the request of the women ministers who every day were in the trenches of dealing with abusive marriages. They lobbied for a marriage course that dealt with this reality and not just the "be open and honest in your communication" stuff.

I asked if the course was the one thing he held onto in his retirement. "I'm not retired, really. I'm a psychologist and still practice downtown. I was a part-time minister."

One night a couple of months before our wedding, Jean and the kids and I were all crammed around the kitchen table. Jean had made pasta and meatballs. For whatever reason, Jean Paul was angry about something or someone.

All I know is that he started yelling and lifting the table. Our pasta and plates slid down to one end.

"Okay, that's it. This ends now!"

Jean Paul could see the anger in Jean's eyes. He put the table down, swore, and started to eat his dinner as if nothing was wrong.

"This family is going into therapy."

Whaaaaaaaaaaaa...?

"Oh Christ. Again?" Jean Paul said.

"I will not put up with this any longer!" Jean answered.

I wasn't quite sure what Jean meant about us all going into therapy. I think she meant as a group, but I didn't dare open my mouth, because it was so very clear that my dog was not in this fight. I had nothing to do with any of this. If anything, I was an injured party. Therapy? I'd had my fill of therapy in treatment. I can assure you, the last thing I needed was more of that. Jean I loved dearly, but her family was ... loud.

Later that night, Jean asked me to find the phone number for the minister who was a psychologist. A week later, all of us were in his office in a downtown tower.

Jean had warned us all to be on time, and it would be worth our lives not to turn up. So, of course, the one person who was late was Jean herself, tied up with patients and running from one thing to the other.

Jean's lateness was such an engrained habit that whenever the kids wanted to bring her to a puddle of regret with a single sentence, they would say, "Mom, you clearly love other people's children more than you do your own — you spend more time with them."

But there we were, all of us surly and unwilling to accept any role in what had clearly been an unaided temper tantrum by Jean Paul.

We had only forty-five minutes with Brian, the therapist. So, he got to work with the same speed and drama as he did at the marriage course. He asked me to stand up. He then asked Jean to stand in front of me and the three kids to stand behind me.

He asked us all if this configuration fairly described our family dynamics.

"Yes," said Jean.

"Sort of," I said.

The kids were silent.

He told me to sit down and turned to the kids. "Is this what your family was like before Bob arrived?"

Yes.

"Is that what you want it to be again?"

No one said a word, but I could tell from their eyes that yeses were on all their lips.

He called me back.

"So now, Bob is blocking you from your mom. And Jean, he's doing the same with you and your kids."

The kids all agreed; Jean didn't say anything.

"I haven't spoken to Bob, but I get a strong sense he's not leaving. Is that right, Bob?"

"Yes."

"And Bob, I bet you're working incredibly hard to get these kids to like you — forget love you — *like* you. Is that right?"

"Uh, well ..."

"And I suspect the harder you try, the harder it gets."

I smiled. "Yes, for sure." Finally, someone understood.

"Well, I have great news for you. I have great news for all of you. Bob, you don't have to work to get them to like you."

This was a surprise. "No?"

"No. Because you're not their father. You're going to be their stepfather. They already have a father. And it's not you. You have one obligation to Jean's children, and one duty only."

I had no idea where he was going with this.

"You have to be civil. That's it. Nothing more. Just be polite."

At that moment, a huge boulder was lifted off my shoulders. *Just be nice?* I thought. *Hell, I can do that.*

And by the look on Jean's and the kids' faces, it looked as if at least some rocks had been lifted from them, as well. Because they didn't have to work around me to get to her.

We left that appointment much happier and "whole-er" than when we'd gone in.

Not all of his wisdom stuck, of course, but it was a brilliant example of how a great teacher can punch through habits and norms that would otherwise fester and hobble everyone whose actions are driven by them. It also let us move forward to our wedding somewhat united as a family.

On July 25, 1993, my best friend and best man, Charles Fremes, had to physically hold me back from the side room at the front of the church where I was peeking through the curtains to look at the many friends waiting for the service to begin.

I'd been brought up with classical music and had spent all those years singing hymns in school. So there was music galore at the service, and not recorded, but live — from the professional banjo player, who strummed "Amazing Grace" in honour of our time on the Appalachian Trail, to a singer from the Canadian Opera Company who made the tears flow with his rendition of "Nessun Dorma," to two trumpeters who belted out "Here Comes the Bride" from the church balcony.

At the point in the service where the Rev. Mary Redner asked, "If anyone here knows any reason why these two people should not be joined in holy matrimony," someone shouted back, "No, hurry up before they change their minds!"

While my parents were long gone and Jean's weren't interested in having a say in the wedding, we couldn't avoid the politics that creep into every wedding everywhere. It came from Jean's medical partner, Carolyn Bennett, who wanted us to have a formal receiving line at the reception, and felt the cake should be cut with a sterling silver knife bought specially for the occasion.

In the end, there was no receiving line, and what cut the wedding cake was the Swiss Army knife I'd used on the Appalachian Trail.

I must say, it was a lovely reception. A hot, sunny Sunday in July, friends old and new, everyone amazed that this was actually happening, no less so than Jean and me. Was it really two years ago that I was in a drug treatment centre in Atlanta?

The time came for speeches. Jean and I would each address the guests, and Jean Paul said he would speak on behalf of himself and his sisters. He'd never spoken in public before, and I prodded Jean to ask him a couple of weeks before the wedding how his speech was coming. He avoided her questions. When she asked the day before the wedding, he refused to tell her. This worried me. I didn't expect him to be Winston Churchill, but I didn't want him to be tongue-tied. I just hoped it was short.

Jean spoke and then invited Jean Paul to the porch overlooking the lawn and the crowd below. I'll never forget his first words: "You know, Bob, when I met you, I really didn't like you."

I froze. Jean's smile disappeared. Everyone was still. My brother Jim, who was standing in the front row, told me after that he thought of faking a heart attack to keep Jean Paul from saying a single word more.

"But then," Jean Paul continued, "I saw that I was wrong. I saw that you really love her. That you're really good for her, and she's good for you, too."

We all breathed again.

He went on, but I can't remember a word he said. I do recall there was tumultuous applause when he was done and that he looked as relieved as I felt.

In the crowd was the ex-wife of a well-known businessman who had also come with his current wife. The two wives hadn't spoken in years. During Jean Paul's speech, they were standing ten yards apart. When he was done, one went over to the other and said, "We should talk."

12 What If Your Mother Married Your Spouse's Father?

As I mentioned, in my first year with Jean there hadn't been a lot of love from her kids.

So in the early months of our relationship, I was trying to learn the opaque rules of being the new man in a mixed family.

Most of all, I was just trying to be nice. I was good at that and it kept me from being yelled at. I had grown up in a household where no one raised their voice, ever.

So to sit around the kitchen table with a family that's half Italian and hear teenagers scream for the pasta was a frightening experience. They didn't look angry. Why were they yelling?

I was told that Thanksgiving dinner was always out in Dunnville, a farming community near Hamilton where Jean's mom and dad lived. I'd heard stories from Jean about blended families and missing siblings but hadn't paid much attention to the cast of characters. All I knew was that her parents were a retired farming couple in their eighties. So Jean and I drove out in my car while the kids went in hers.

Jean's mom was very hospitable and easy to talk to. Jean's dad, not so much. He seemed openly hostile to me. I couldn't figure this out. I was being the politest guest I could possibly be and he was clearly having none of it. Had Jean told him of my drug use? Had the kids?

On the drive back to Toronto, I mentioned this to Jean. She looked oddly at me, which I thought odd in itself.

"You didn't listen to me, did you?"

"What do you mean?"

"When I told you the stories about my parents."

"Uh ..."

Again, I seem to have broken some rule I didn't know was there.

"Manny isn't my father. He's Rene's father."

Rene (as in Guarino) was her ex-husband.

"Uh ..."

"Did it not strike you as odd that their name is Marmoreo, which is my *married* name?"

Of course I'd never thought of any of this. But if it was true, then Jean's mother appeared to be married to her ex-husband's father.

Now it all made sense. Of course the man I thought was Jean's dad wasn't thrilled to see the man who had replaced his son in his own home. I got it. What I didn't get was how this bizarre marriage came to be. I mean, can you imagine *your* mother marrying your spouse's father?

But so it was here and now. Mary Bradt and Manny Marmoreo knew each other, of course. They'd been in-laws for seventeen years.

After Jean's marriage broke up with Rene, these two people who'd lost their spouses stayed in touch. The short version of this story is that while Manny and Mary knew each other, his family was worried because he'd got himself involved with "the wrong kind of woman," who not only swore but drank Scotch. So Jean and Rene concocted a plan to send Manny to spend a few days at Mary's in Dunnville where she lived. Mary was involved with three different seniors' groups, all of whom loved to travel, and her job was to introduce Manny to each of these groups in the hope that he would find a more suitable mate.

They sent Manny to see Mary on the pretense of helping her get a dead cat out of her well. They both drove him out and told him he should feel free to stay for a few days. This was to give Mary time to introduce him to the Other Women. But he called the next day and asked to be taken home.

Uh-oh, what happened? Manny wasn't talking.

But a week later, Mary called Jean and said, "I'm just here in Toronto visiting Manny."

That was one shoe dropping.

The next was six months later when Jean was visiting Mary in Dunnville. Mary thrust her hand in Jean's face and said, "Look at my finger." There it was — her wedding ring.

By all accounts, Mary and Manny had a wonderful marriage. But by a decade later, they'd fallen victim to the thousand natural shocks that flesh is heir to.

One morning in 2003, Jean took Mary to St. Joseph's Hospital in Hamilton, where she was to have surgery. Jean's sister, Joyce, would drive Manny into Hamilton to see Mary after she got out of the recovery room.

But just as the nurses were wheeling Mary into the operating theatre, Jean's cellphone rang. It was a neighbour in Dunnville. There was an ambulance outside Manny's house. It seemed Manny had just had a heart attack. They were taking him to Dunnville Hospital.

Jean hung up as the doors to the surgical theatre closed behind Mary. Jean called Manny's doctor and asked what's going on. He told her it was very bad. Manny was now at the hospital but would likely not survive the morning.

Jean then called me (I was at work in my office in Toronto) and told me to call Rene and tell him his father was dying in Dunnville and that he was to get there as soon as possible. She hung up.

I'd never met Jean's ex. But I knew he worked for Maclaren, the big advertising agency. So I called them and asked for Rene Marmoreo. The receptionist told me he was in a meeting. "It's a family emergency," I said. "Please get him out of the meeting."

"Who shall I say is calling?"

"Bob Ramsay."

"And you're family?"

The briefest pause. "Yes, yes, I am."

A few seconds later Rene Marmoreo came on the line.

"Hi, it's Bob Ramsay. Jean told me to tell you that she's with Mary who's having surgery in Hamilton and that Manny's just had a heart attack and that you're to get to Dunnville Hospital right now because he likely won't survive the morning."

"Okay."

And that was that.

As it turned out, Rene did manage to get to Dunnville just minutes before his father died. Meanwhile, Mary was out of surgery and in the recovery room.

Jean and her sister, Joyce, huddled, waiting for Mary to wake from the anaesthetic and see her husband standing there. They decided to delay telling her, giving some excuse that he'd be there later. They were afraid the shock (she was eighty-nine, after all) would kill her.

About an hour later, Mary awoke from her groggy sleep, slowly took in Jean and Joyce who were at her bedside, looked around the room, and said, "He's dead, isn't he?"

13 Burying the Truth

My two half-brothers and half-sister — all from my dad's first marriage, before the Second World War — are fifteen to twenty years older than I am, so my siblings were more like distant uncles and an aunt when I was growing up. But after my mom died in 1969 from atherosclerosis, my dad was soon diagnosed with prostate cancer. This brought the four of us together in a new way.

Back then, cancer was still something you didn't talk about openly, and none of us felt close enough to our father to ask, "How long do you think you have left?" Because, again, back then cancer was something you died from, not lived with. Our biggest concern after Mom died was that Dad was wandering around all alone in our big home in Edmonton.

We all tried to push him into moving into a condominium, but he wouldn't budge. And who's to blame him? That's where his life had been for thirty years. His harpsichord, which he had lovingly constructed, was there. His books. His habits.

We all took turns travelling back to Edmonton and asking him to visit us in Toronto and B.C., and a couple of times we took him on trips to England and the U.S. During the next two years, he developed an odd habit: he would take out the financial statements for Walter Ramsay Florists and go through them, line by line, so we would know what it was worth (and in many ways what his worth as a father was) when the time came for us to sell the business after he'd died. None of us wanted to become florists, so it had to be either sold or shuttered.

By late 1972 we knew Dad's health was failing by reports from Edmonton friends and from my own recent visit where he looked to be at normal weight. This was cause for alarm because he'd been stout all his life.

In early January of 1973, we got the call. Dad had fallen and been taken to hospital. His prostate cancer had spread to his brain. He had weeks, possibly days, to live. We all headed to Edmonton and our dying father. I was the first to arrive. Ironically, he was in a room at the Edmonton General Hospital that was next door to the room my mom had lingered in for months before she died two years earlier.

I asked the doctor what the prognosis was. He was young, curt, and spoke only in medical terms. I was twenty-two, terrified, and afraid to ask more. Not that more Q & A would have solved anything. The doctor said something about "a couple of weeks at most" and I had all the information I needed.

My older half-brothers, Peter and Jim, and half-sister, Joan, all arrived the next day. Naturally, they asked me for a detailed summary of my conversation with the doctor. The most insistent was Jim, the oldest, gruffest, and the one I was to learn had a morbid fear of hospitals and death. So during our collective death watch, he stayed away and asked me to fill him in, something I was completely incapable of doing except to say that Dad's sleeping a lot and they're giving him drugs for his pain. We brought in a small record player so we could play him his beloved symphonies.

We made sure that one of us was always there in the room with him. Always.

I couldn't imagine what it would be like to die alone, with your absent children not there when you breathed your last. So we set up three eight-hour watches around the clock, sleeping in his room, darting down to the basement cafeteria for our meals. I was on watch one afternoon after Dad had nodded off to sleep. The nurses had said he had a couple of days at most. My sister, Joan, wasn't due for an hour, so I ducked out for a coffee and by the time I got back ten minutes later ...

Dad had died.

Oh my God! Oh Christ, no! What have I done?!

A doctor and two nurses were in his room. They didn't have to say anything. Their looks told it all.

They made way for me as I rushed to the bed, my father's eyes shut, his face pale and still.

I was drenched in guilt. My only job was to be there for him and I had left him in his moment of greatest need — to get a coffee!

My father had died alone. No, it was worse than that. He died *because* I left his bedside. I abandoned him and killed him. What sin can a son commit that's worse than that?

But worse than that, I'd let down my brothers and sister — whom I'd never really proven my worth to. Here I was, the youngest, playing at being their leader. How utterly vain of me.

Theirs was a simple request, to be there for our father. In fact, it was one that I had insisted on. And who was the one to break that sacred pact?

Me.

I asked to use the phone at the nursing station and called my sister, Joanie, who was waiting at home.

"Dad's died."

"Oh, I'm so sorry, Bob. Was he —?"

"Yes, he was asleep. The nurse came in to take his pulse and …"

I started to cry.

"Oh, I'm so glad you were there."

"Me, too."

We buried my father next to my mother two days later on a brutally cold January day in Edmonton. The only thing I remember about the funeral is that the hearse got stuck in a snowbank on the way from the church to the cemetery and we all had to pile out of the family car behind and help dig it out.

The next day, the four of us were walking from the lawyer's office to Dad's flower shop downtown when Joanie said, "It's cold. Why don't we go in somewhere and have a drink and warm up?"

I said sure because it was bloody cold, and I didn't really think about how this was a first for us: we were not a family that ever went "for a drink to warm up." We ducked into a bar on Jasper Avenue.

We talked about Dad's illness and concluded that he didn't die of cancer; he died of a broken heart. After Mom's death two years earlier, the life had gone out of him. I know lots of people say this looking back on their parents' lives and deaths.

But I remember the day after Dad died, I was looking through one of his filing cabinets in the den at home. There was a Valentine's

Day card that said: "To Ede, all my love forever. Valentine's 1970."
Mom had died the year before.

After our drinks were served, Joanie turned to me and said,
"Bob, you know how Dad's estate is divided four ways?"

"Sure."

"Well, we're kind of wondering" — here she gestured to Jim and
Peter — "what you'd think if we divided it five ways instead?"

"Five ways? Why?"

"Because you have another sister."

Maybe I was just dumb with grief at my father's funeral the day
before. Maybe because I was slow to figure out that my siblings had
engineered this whole encounter. But I didn't feel shocked or even
angry that this secret had been kept from me until now, when I was
twenty-two. I just felt numb.

There's not much I remember with pinpoint accuracy those
many years ago. But I do remember the next ten minutes
precisely.

What I felt was a huge need to feel something, anything. I also
felt I should be feeling one of two things because this is the kind of
situation where I would either feel that I wanted to rush into the
arms of my long-lost half-sister, or I wanted to have nothing to do
with any of my half-siblings.

I learned she was the child of my father's first wife, as were the
three others.

I still didn't get it. Why was she a secret?

Then Joanie told me our dad and his first wife were having such
a bitter breakup brought about by her affair with his commanding
officer in the dying days of World War II that Dad had disowned
that child — even though she *was* their child.

My gentle, puttering, old dad had disowned his daughter?
Banished her from the family because she was the child not only of
him, but of his faithless wife? How incredibly angry must he have

been to do that? But these questions only bubbled up days later, and I quickly stuffed them away.

It turns out she had been put up for "private adoption" to a Vancouver family, which happened a lot after World War II. Joanie had stayed in touch with her and was the conduit of information to her two full brothers. And clearly, in all the nearly thirty years since, my father hadn't softened his view, hadn't picked up the phone and asked to speak to his daughter, whose only sin was that she was the offspring of him and his first wife.

Later on, I wondered how enraged you must be to do something like that — and to not waver in your rage for the rest of your life.

But on that day in that bar, I simply said, "Sure, let's divide the will into five parts."

I never really thought about her after that day, though I did meet her the night before the wedding of one of my nieces, the daughter of my sister, Joanie, who knew about her "step-aunt" and treated her as the member of the family that she was.

It was the rehearsal dinner at a hotel in Whistler. We each knew the other would be there. We hugged awkwardly, chit-chatted for ten minutes until someone interrupted us, and parted ways.

Oh, and there was someone else of note at that rehearsal dinner. My father's first wife. She was now very old, but as I watched her "receive" all her clan and close friends of the bride and groom, I saw that she was the queen of appearances. I went up to her and introduced myself. She nodded her head, recognizing that I was the only child of her ex-husband's second marriage. And then she smiled and turned to speak to someone else.

Meanwhile, Jean was seated on a couch, watching all this and trying to construct the family genogram, something family physicians do instinctively. But she was having a very hard time getting mine straight in her head.

14 The Birth of JeansMarines

There's an odd upside to not knowing what you're doing. You're not afraid of what everyone who does know what they're doing has reason to fear.

Our three months hiking on the Appalachian Trail had made us superbly fit. It would be a shame to let all that go to seed. If anything, our time together on the Trail had made us confident we could do pretty much anything if we put our minds to it. If we could do it alone on the Trail, it would be even better to do it with thirty-five thousand other people in the city. *The* city. And if it took the better part of a day rather than a summer ... well, that's how we talked ourselves into entering the 1994 New York City Marathon. I was forty-four and Jean fifty-one.

No online applications in those days. So when the letter came saying we were accepted, we thought we'd better do some training before the last week of October when those runners take over all five boroughs of the city and two million New Yorkers cheer us wildly on. Yes, two million people yelling, "Go, Bob, Go!" Who would deny himself that?

We knew we had to get in shape. Beyond that, we knew nothing. We didn't join a training group, or even buy a book on the subject. We got ready for New York the way we did for the Appalachian Trail, by making up our own program and hoping it worked. We didn't know what we didn't know.

But Jean heard somewhere that you should run four out of five weekdays, starting with a mile run and gradually building up to five miles over the six months you need to train.

Then on weekends, do one long run on either Saturday or Sunday and take the other day off. Add a mile a week until you peak at 26.2 miles, or 42.2 kilometres — the full distance of a marathon — three weeks before the marathon. Oh, and drink a lot of water and look both ways when you cross the street.

So that's what we did. Early on we took the lessons of persistence we learned on the Trail and applied them to marathon training. Like, run earlier in the day, if you can. That way, and especially if you're a doctor, there's less chance your patient obligations will trample your resolution. And if you do have to skip a day, for sure don't skip two in a row. That's an invitation to be a sideliner.

Speaking of persistence, it's far easier when you're not alone, a lesson I learned from recovery. So Jean and I would try to head out together as often as we could. Back then, we'd finish apart because I was faster than she was. That would change dramatically over time.

All to say, it's harder to go back to sleep at 6:00 a.m. when you don't have someone waiting to meet you on the corner for your buddy-run.

On a sunny Saturday in September, my program finally called for me to run 26.2 miles through the streets of Toronto. I had my route planned out in my head. I had lots of protein bars and a waterbelt full of water. Plus cash to get Gatorade along the route or to grab a cab home if I injured myself or couldn't go the distance.

As I left the house at eight that morning, I spotted Jean Paul in the den watching TV. He was seventeen at the time.

"Hey, J-P, whatcha doing?"

"Watchin' TV."

"Oh ya?"

"Uh-huh."

He never turned his head from the screen.

"I'm going for a run."

"Ya?"

"Ya, I'm going to run a marathon."

"Uh-huh."

"All 26.2 miles of it."

"Ya?"

"You know how far that is?"

"Twenty-six point two miles. You said."

"I meant how far 26.2 miles is."

Silence.

"It's the distance from the Four Seasons in Yorkville to the Ford Assembly Plant in Oakville."

Silence.

"Pretty far, eh?"

"Ya."

"See ya."

"Ya."

I could see I was making real progress in bringing Jean's kids into my world.

So out the door I went and four hours later, as I was heading into my last six miles, I got what every runner dreams of: a runner's high.

Suddenly, as I was running east along Eglinton Avenue, there were stars in my eyes. Yes, bright little lights that blinked. Really. At the same time, when I should have felt tired and plodding, I had an amazing surge of energy. For four blocks I felt like dancing down the street. I could have run forever, and the stars made me feel even more light-headed. It didn't last, of course, and my last mile was real agony. But I'd done it: I'd run a marathon before running The Marathon. Knowing I could go the distance took a huge weight off my shoulders. But the addict in me wanted to know if I ran a marathon every day, would I still get high and see stars? Maybe there was a way I could carve out four more hours plus every day and ... No? Okay. But a guy can dream.

Our plane landed at LaGuardia the Friday afternoon before the big race on the third Sunday in October. As we came over a hill toward midtown in our cab, all of Manhattan came into view. Way to the south was the World Trade Center, and "twice as south" we could barely make out the Verrazzano Bridge, where the race would start. Oh. My. God. What had we got ourselves into? It was impossibly far. The route called for runners to cross from Brooklyn into Manhattan on the 59th Street Bridge, then head uptown on First Avenue (where a million people would be lining the street) to 138th Street in the Bronx, then roll down Fifth Avenue to the Plaza Hotel on 59th Street, turn right, and head back into Central Park and the finish line at the Tavern on the Green.

At dinner the night before the race, Jean reached down in her purse, drew out a pillbox, took out a small yellow pill, and said, "Take this tomorrow just before the race."

"Is it an Advil?"

"Honey, it's ten Advils."

Talk about peer pressure. She's my wife, and a doctor, and I'm an addict. How could I say no? I did as I was told and finished my first marathon pain-free.

The next morning, we took a cab to as close as we could get on Staten Island to the start line on the bridge. We were still a mile away where he let us off. The crowds were that big. Waves and waves of people poured off buses and out of cars into the staging areas. We had an hour to go before the starter's pistol fired and thirty-three thousand very fit people began a journey that could last as little as a bit over two hours or as long as six or eight. Giant marathons like New York, London, and Boston are rare athletic events where one participant can set a world record and another can take all day to finish.

Thousands of us waited at a former army base at the foot of the bridge to be herded into our corrals. Jean and I were separated early on, with women starting away from men. We agreed to meet at the front door of the Tavern on the Green after the race. Meanwhile, half a dozen helicopters flew overhead and scores of boats waited below the bridge to see the start. Police barked instructions and pretty much everyone used one of the hundreds of portaloos. I got acquainted with what I found out later is the world's longest pissoir. It was there that I said to the man next to me, "Is this your first New York?"

"This is my twelfth."

"Really? Where are you from?"

"Poland."

"Wow, that's quite the trip."

"Yep, every year. It's a reunion."

"And your finish time?" This is every marathoner's obsession.

"About two hours later than I should."

"Oh, how so?"

"Because there's a bar at 73rd and First. Check it out when you go by. There's a guy standing on a painters' ladder so we can see him.

He's Polish, too. We all paint houses. So we all stop in at the bar for a beer and corn beef. That adds one hour. The other hour comes from trying to run after a couple of beers."

I was impressed. "How many in your group?"

"This year, twenty."

Soon, we were called to the start and waited and fretted for the starter's gun to go off. The elite runners were in the first two rows. They would finish the race in half the time we tried to. Behind them was a row of runners from the NYPD and fire department who would link arms to create a wall that made it impossible for an ordinary runner to sprint out in front at the start for their ten seconds of fame with the news cameras of the world.

Just before I got on the bridge, someone handed me a Magic Marker and said I should write my name and city on the front of my T-shirt so the crowd could cheer me on by name and hometown. For the next 26.2 miles and four hours and twelve minutes, the sound of "Go, Bob!" "Yea … Toronto!" rang in my ears.

There were blind people running. People in wheelchairs. Soldiers in full pack gear.

I came up behind a guy who was … could it really be? … naked. Almost. He was wearing a flesh-coloured thong. But he and pretty much everyone else in New York that brisk fall day were having the time of their lives.

When I ran down Fifth Avenue, turned right at the Plaza, and headed into Central Park and the finish line, the crowds were still huge, even though the winner had finished two hours before.

I crossed the finish line at Tavern on the Green with arms raised high in triumph. I'd run 26.2 miles in four hours and twelve minutes. I was exhausted and delirious with joy. Volunteers put a medal around my neck, thrust Gatorade and pretzels into my hands. Wrapped a space blanket around me so I wouldn't chill down.

It took about a minute for me to decide I wanted to do this next year. Only faster. The race. The city. The crowds. The world. It was all there for me. This was the real runner's high.

I met Jean half an hour later, as planned. She felt pretty much like I did. And as we walked the forty blocks in the fading light through Central Park back to our hotel, we were abuzz with the people we ran with, the stories we'd heard, and the chance to be part of a huge band of people who gather to celebrate life in such an extraordinary way.

So was born our love of destination marathons.

For the next three years, we ran New York.

But having run it the dumb way once, we vowed henceforth to be a lot smarter. We read books, swallowed running magazines whole, and for my birthday Jean got me a running coach. Erin Hogan met me two mornings a week and upped my pace gradually and insistently.

I finished my second New York Marathon twenty-five minutes faster than my first.

Erin said, "You should qualify for Boston."

One reason the Boston Marathon is the most famous race on earth is that you have to qualify in order to apply, let alone get accepted. And in the midnineties, the number of people running these big-city marathons — whether Paris, or Tokyo, or Boston — was shooting up. New York had become so popular that they rejected every other applicant. Having thirty-five thousand people running down a street can stretch all kinds of city services. Having seventy thousand people is an invitation to breakdown.

But Boston has always held itself apart. Just to qualify, you had to finish in a certain time within your five-year age and gender group at another accredited marathon. Or if you ran Boston once, you could use your time to re-qualify for next year. Back in 1996, if you were a male between forty-five and fifty, your qualifying time for Boston was three hours, thirty-five minutes. (For Boston in 2020, it's three hours and twenty minutes. Yikes!) So throughout 1996 I trained and worked and ate and drank with one goal in mind: to do New York in 3:35. The race that year wasn't much fun because I was so single-mindedly focused on my goal. I bought a nifty runner's watch to chart every mile — only to see it blow out of my hands at the start on the bridge and fall to its death in the Hudson far below. But that was okay, because I also wrote my split times on my arms. That was not okay as my sweat soon turned all those numbers to mush.

I crossed the finish line in 3:41 — my fastest time yet, but six minutes slower than what I needed to qualify for Boston.

I gave up on Boston because I'd spent so much time trying to qualify — and clearly would need to spend even more time next year training to cut those six terrible minutes off my time — that I decided it wasn't worth the candle.

But while I was getting faster, Jean was getting slower. This made sense since she was now fifty-four years old, not an age at which many women anywhere were running marathons. She also kept getting injured, and in the 1997 edition of New York, she had to hobble her final mile to make it to the finish.

We decided we'd keep running marathons but do it in different cities. The next year we ran Long Beach, and the year after, San Antonio. But I had to withdraw from that marathon at Mile 4 because of a pulled muscle. By 2001, I'd added a bad back to my ailments.

Despite this, I entered us into the Marine Corps Marathon that October in Washington. It too is a big marathon, with twenty-five thousand runners, and it's organized entirely by the U.S. Marine Corps. We weren't at all sure we'd be up for it when the time came. But it was good to know we could if the pressure eased up on us in the fall.

Then on September 11, 2001, planes flew into the World Trade Center and the Pentagon.

Like everyone, we were transfixed by the tragedy. I was in New York on 9/11, Jean was at our cottage writing. The night before, I told her I was going to be having meetings "downtown" the next day. That morning she was panic-stricken. I scored what must have been the last rental car in Manhattan that day, stashed it in a parking lot overnight, and headed home the next day. When I got to the Canadian border at Gananoque, I could see things had changed already. There, on the Canadian side, was an RCMP car with two Mounties standing outside carrying shotguns. When I got home that night, Jean and I hugged and cried and we gorged on hamburgers and fries with the kids.

I don't really know what got us on the plane six weeks later to run the Marine Corps in Washington. I really was in a lot of pain when I ran, and Jean's work and book obligations had put training a distant third.

I think we wanted to honour all those people who'd died. And it was a fitting way to end our marathon careers: we'd just have to think of some other extreme endurance sport to keep us fit and visit some more great cities.

Washington was completely different from New York. There were more helicopters in the air. But they weren't news helicopters; they were Marine helicopters. The crowds weren't as big. But they were hugely patriotic, waving American flags and spontaneously breaking out into "The Star-Spangled Banner."

Of course, 9/11 had a lot to do with it. Even our route was changed to go around the Pentagon twice. So we'd all be sure to see the huge hole in the side of it. The runners were just as hyper-patriotic. Running under an underpass, they'd scream, "We're Number One! We're Number One!" At one point as we rounded the Pentagon, a crewcutted man in his fifties running in front of me appeared to stumble and fall. I veered to avoid running into him. I glanced back and saw that he wasn't hurt; he was just praying.

All of this had its effect, because nobody does patriotism better than the Americans. It took me until Mile 25, when I could see the finish line at the Iwo Jima Memorial near Arlington Cemetery, to notice that I'd run the entire race in no pain.

Pain had been part of me, part of every training run in the past year. Where did it go? I was watching for it at the start, hoping I could make it more than my four measly miles in San Antonio the year before. But then I got diverted by the growing feeling that I wasn't running a marathon; I was participating in a rite of passage.

When I crossed the finish line, a big, strapping U.S. Marine hung a medal around my neck. I knew I had thirty minutes to kill waiting for Jean. But I could get my Gatorade and pretzels and space blanket and just walk around the Iwo Jima Memorial with its iconic statue of Marines raising the U.S. flag.

"Hey, stranger."

It was Jean.

"Honey, what are you doing here? You aren't due for another twenty, thirty minutes."

"I did well."

"You finished?"

"Of course I did."

"What was your time?"

"Four ten."

She'd finished one minute faster than me.

"You sure did. Wow!"

As we walked back to our hotel in Georgetown, we recounted all the incredible sights we'd seen along the route, including a young female private whose rifle seemed to be taller than she was, and the Marine veteran in the crowd who yelled at Jean, "Lady, you're my hero!" (*Are you kidding me?* she'd thought.)

Then Jean casually said, "You know, next year we should bring some friends."

And that is how JeansMarines was born.

15 The Glorious Rise and Calamitous Fall of JeansMarines

JeansMarines was a crazy idea right from the start.

We began by holding "information sessions" in our condo, where a coach from the Running Room told our friends that anyone could run a marathon. You just had to get out there and train.

The audience was our friends, mainly women, nearly all middle-aged, and definitely not in great physical shape. We'd twisted their arms to come and hear about this impossibility, then twisted some more as we gushed about the idea that they could move from the couch to the finish line in just six months.

So was born what grew into the largest women's marathon group in North America at the time. By 2005, over four hundred JeansMarines did the Marine Corps Marathon in Washington, D.C.

Jean and I are no fans of those weekend retreats that promise to make you a new and better person. JeansMarines took six months of hard physical training, plus the 26.2 miles of the actual marathon. Over that half year, its members created extraordinarily strong bonds. We even had a family-lawyer-in-residence who handled the many divorces that took place as these women said, "Hey, he's still on the couch. The kids are gone. I'm not going to just hang around here for another thirty years."

By 2005, JeansMarines had grown into a thrilling monster — we had a full-time manager, non-profit status, and five satellite operations across Toronto.

I had the heady high of dreaming of expanding across Canada ... into the U.S. ... the world!

JeansMarines was an idea whose time had come.

Nothing could stop us. That October, more JeansMarines had crossed the finish line in Washington than ever — some three hundred women and a few good men.

Some didn't cross, of course, because they were too slow to "make the bridge." Runners had to cross the 14th Street Bridge by a certain time to be allowed to continue the remaining six miles to the finish line and collect their medal. The Marines imposed this rule because you can't keep a major Washington artery closed indefinitely just so a few stragglers can get a medal.

This has been a grey area in the race. Some years, if you didn't make the bridge you were out of the race, couldn't continue, and, most important, couldn't get your medal. And believe me, this was all about getting that medal — and the hug from the Marine at the finish line.

But other years, you could board a Marine bus at one end of the bridge, which would let you off at the other, where you could continue in the race, finish it, and get that medal.

In still other years, the Marine bus would pick you up and drive you to the finish line, but you wouldn't get back in the race, couldn't cross the finish line, and couldn't collect your medal. It all seemed to be up to the bus driver.

Each year, our collective time as a group was getting slower and slower, as more and more walkers joined JeansMarines. Jean and I disagreed over this: Jean felt any woman should be able to join and train and do the 26.2 miles, no matter how she finished. I felt that if you couldn't even finish what you'd devoted nine months of your life to preparing for, there's a flaw somewhere.

Sadly, the need for our people to get that medal led to our cheating in order to get it.

That last sentence is a testament to how desperately important some participants made crossing the line. I'm not talking about cheating in order to win the marathon, to place first; I'm talking about cheating in order to finish it, to place at all.

It seems we weren't the first. In the past, we'd hear of "the short-cut," where participants would cut off the route and join up again close to the bridge. This cut about two miles from their race and let a whole lot more of them get to the bridge before the Marines closed it. In 2004, I noticed some walkers taking the shortcut, including some JeansMarines. Back at the hotel after that race, Jean mentioned that she'd told the slower JeansMarines about the short-cut. I was upset because ... well first, I have to admit, because I was afraid that they'd get caught, and then — and only then — that it was cheating.

The morning of the race in 2005, Jean mentioned that she'd again told some of our slowest members to take the shortcut. This time, I really did get upset, but now it was because I was shocked that Jean could still think this was right. The word *values* didn't enter the conversation, but that's what it was clearly all about.

That day, about a dozen JeansMarines took the shortcut, "finished," and collected their medals. A week after our celebration dinner back in Toronto following the race, I got an email from a woman who'd been a spectator, had seen some of our women taking the shortcut, and was asking if this was right.

I didn't reply. We were invincible, and who was this person?

She politely wrote again asking if Jean or JeansMarines had anything to say.

I didn't reply. I thought she would go away.

Pride cometh before the fall.

A few days later, the *Globe and Mail* had an investigative piece in the Saturday paper laying out the cheating scandal. Only then did we react. Jean apologized publicly. We offered to turn back our medals to the marathon organizers, even though they didn't ask for them. We were banned from the Marine Corps Marathon for a year.

It was a devastating blow. While many JeansMarines from years past and present rallied to our aid, some were scathing. Journalist Christie Blatchford, a JeansMarine from Year One, wrote a column chronicling our collective arrogance and malfeasance. One even mailed us a JeansMarines T-shirt covered in dog poo.

I was angry with Jean for letting her desire to help "her women" across the finish warp her own values and boundaries. Somehow, she thought that a shortcut into last place was different from a shortcut into first place. I was angrier still that she seemed to recover much faster from the "shunning" than I did.

The truth is, there really wasn't any "shunning," except in my head.

For months I walked around anticipating … well, I'm not sure what. A blow? A snide remark? While Jean just got on with her life, I carried around the guilt of … Well, I hadn't taken the shortcut, but it was a testament to how much I'd invested my own identity into JeansMarines that I stayed hobbled for so long.

True, we did go back in 2007 to run the Marine Corps Marathon. But it was never the same. We spent more time helping fewer people. One night in 2008, we took the subway out to Scarborough for a recruiting session in a public library branch. It turned out that there were the two of us — and two potential recruits. That's when we decided to close down JeansMarines. After the 2008 post-race celebration, not with 350 women in a hotel banquet room, but with 35 in our condo, we told the JeansMarines the news. There were lots of tears that night. But for Jean and me, lots of relief, too.

We could get on with our lives and not try to revive what couldn't be revived.

Little did I know that for Jean this would mean running more — and running faster.

16 "The Last Time I Was Here, I Died."

By 2006, I wore my street cred in the world of adventure like a medal.

Five years before, I'd finished running my tenth marathon and was in the best shape of my life. We'd trekked to Mt. Everest, hiked a thousand miles of the Appalachian Trail, sea kayaked in the High Arctic.

JeansMarines had taken hundreds of women off the couch and trained them to do the Marine Corps Marathon. Jean had gone on to be the fastest woman in her age group in the Boston Marathon.

But one day in 2005 I had asked my family doctor if I could have a stress echocardiogram. I did it more out of cockiness than caution. I just wanted to have proof of how fit my heart was.

But, as I was to find out, fit doesn't mean healthy. That test and the events that followed would teach me some painful lessons about what we can and can't control in our lives. The stress echo revealed that I had a heart murmur. It seems that one in a hundred Canadians is born with one, and, as with half the cases, I'd need to come back — in my case, in ten to fifteen years — and get a new aortic valve.

My only concern was whether I'd be able to run after I got that new valve. "Of course you can run," my cardiologist assured me. That was in 2006.

By January 2011, I was barely able to walk up stairs without stopping for breath. I'd "nap" for an hour in the morning at work, and for another hour in the afternoon. One day I went to a gym to do some spinning on a bike and had to quit after one minute.

Jean grew alarmed.

More tests came in rapid order. My aortic valve was wearing out much sooner than expected. My cardiologist said I already needed valve replacement surgery. So on May 3, 2011, my rib cage was cut open, my heart was bypassed, and a team of surgeons at the Peter Munk Cardiac Centre at the Toronto General Hospital replaced my aging aortic valve with a shiny new titanium one.

All went well. Right after surgery, I was taken to the intensive care unit for twenty-four hours. I was expected to remain in hospital for another four or five days. Then I'd be sent home and for the next six weeks or so, I'd recuperate, and walk a little farther each day. I could look forward to being back at work in a couple of months. When I was feeling up to it, I could ride my bike or even run.

That day in intensive care I drifted in and out of consciousness. The nurses asked me endlessly if I knew what day it was and could I spell the word *world* backwards. Jean was by my side. Once when I woke up, she looked teary. I asked her what was wrong.

"Well, honey, you didn't have a near-death experience."

What was she talking about?

"You had a death experience."

"What do you mean?"

She was looking steadily into my eyes. "Your heart stopped."

"What!?"

I first thought it was a bad joke. I have to admit my next thought was "Wow, I'm invincible!" Then after a few seconds of silence as I absorbed the impact of what Jean had said, I burst into tears.

As I wept, Jean told me I'd had sudden "heart block," where the electrical signals from one part of my heart to another suddenly shut down.

"How long was I dead?"

"About three minutes."

"How did they restart my heart?"

"Just like on television."

So the next day, I had a pacemaker inserted below my collarbone to kick-start my heart should it ever "block" again.

F. Scott Fitzgerald once said that in the real dark night of the soul, it is always three o'clock in the morning. For me, it was five o'clock. At that hour, when everything in the hospital is at its most dark and quiet, I would wake from my drugged sleep and cry.

I know people die on the operating table. For every one hundred Canadians who undergo aortic replacement surgery, 2.7 will not make it (although at the Munk Cardiac Centre the rate is 0.9 percent).

Our aged parents can die in surgery, maybe. Not us. And certainly not *me*. Besides, I'd survived the open-heart surgery with flying colours. Mind you, I couldn't remember a single thing about dying or coming back from the dead. No flashing lights or smiling loved ones. Nothing.

In fact, I had to take it entirely on faith that any of this had happened at all.

I told myself that my job right now was to get better physically. Over the next six weeks, I tried to do precisely that. At home, I read a lot of books, watched too much TV drama, and walked a little farther each day.

Jean didn't say much about my death beyond commenting occasionally that life hangs by a thread. All doctors know this first-hand. They deal with it every day. Which may be why they don't mention it much. I also know that for Jean, this was a matter of "You didn't die. Your operation worked. Now get better."

17 A Heart Goes Haywire

Two months after my surgery, Jean and I met with my cardiac surgeon, who pronounced my open-heart surgery a total success. There was a bounce in my step as we left his office, Jean walking up University Avenue to her clinic and me downtown to a client meeting, both of us relieved that life would now get back to normal.

I ducked in to the Hilton Hotel to the men's room on the lower floor. Suddenly, my legs buckled. I grabbed ahold of the railing. What the hell was that?

I felt light-headed. My hands and jaw started to tingle. My lips grew numb. I turned around and pulled myself up the stairs to the main floor. I was damned if I was going to die alone in the men's room in the basement of a hotel.

I walked unsteadily into the lobby and sat down. By this time, I was feeling dizzy, but I had to get out of there. So I got up and walked, one foot slowly in front of the other, outside. The doorman looked at me oddly. I was walking like a drunken sailor.

When I walked smack into a building, hitting my arm on the marble wall, I knew I was in trouble. I was having a stroke. I had to get to the hospital. It had to be Toronto General. They had all my records.

It was six blocks away.

Somehow, I managed to walk out onto the street and into oncoming traffic. I raised my hand and a taxi stopped right away. I got into the back and said, "Toronto General Emerg."

The driver looked at me in his mirror: "Are you okay, mister?"

"I'm not sure."

Three minutes later, we were at the front door of the largest emergency unit in Canada. I struggled out of the cab and managed to walk up to the reception. I blurted out, "I'm having a stroke."

By now, I was pouring sweat and barely able to stand. Within one minute, two triage nurses got me into an examining room. There, they asked me if I could talk, if I was in pain, if I felt numb and where ("My hands, my jaw!") and even the old standby, if I could spell the word *world* backwards. The waves of dizziness forced me to prop my head on the top of my chair as I tried to answer their questions.

The nurses moved me into an acute care cardio bed in the ER. They called Jean, who rushed over. Over the next three hours, all kinds of doctors, nurses, and technicians poked, probed, and questioned me. I felt better lying down, but the waves of dizziness and rapid heartbeat kept coming every fifteen minutes. I was terrified.

A couple of times in the months before my heart surgery I'd felt dizzy and had to sit down, and when Jean took my pulse, she had declared I was in atrial fibrillation. In other words, I had an occasional irregular heartbeat, with resulting palpitations and shortness of breath.

It turns out my heart had remained in Afib after the surgery. I just didn't know it, because you can be in Afib and feel fine (though your risk for stroke can be dangerously high), or you can be in Afib and feel like you're having a stroke and a heart attack at the same time.

This had been my first real Afib attack. As a precaution after the surgery, the doctors had prescribed a strong beta blocker called metoprolol to stop an attack like this. Unfortunately, it had made me tired and lethargic. In other words, pretty much as I felt before surgery.

After an hour in the ER, I was struck by the fact that no one was using the word *stroke* anymore, so I assumed I wasn't having one. It seems I had had a particularly virulent Afib attack that had broken through the metoprolol and sent my heartbeat racing — irregularly — to 140 beats per minute. All the doctors could do for now was give me more metoprolol.

Six hours later, feeling exhausted and relieved, I left the ER with Jean. We took a cab home and I was well and truly gorked on metoprolol.

The next morning, Jean told me my new prescription for metoprolol would double the dose of what I'd been taking. Even though it would make me feel even more lethargic, I should stay on the high dosage until they figured out what to do. I was so tired I could hardly work, had to sleep during the day, and felt tired after even twelve hours' sleep at night.

Clearly, my Afib was no longer a benign condition. I learned that a third of all strokes are caused by it.

While I'd hoped to be back to work within weeks of surgery, I now realized it would take me longer to recover. Just writing a brief email took enormous energy. My concentration was shot, and my memory ... well, it leaked everywhere.

Jean said a lot of this was because of the drugs I was on and she was right. But even talking was tiring; a ten-minute conversation would leave me drained and mute. And though I gradually got my strength and focus back over those weeks, if someone had asked me to write a thirty-minute speech, as I'd routinely done before, I no longer had it in me.

A week after my first Afib attack, it struck again. This time, I had a foreboding. Walking along Bay Street in midtown Toronto, I suddenly felt very light-headed. I knew right away I'd have to lie down, so I walked as fast as I could back to my office. I unlocked the door and then bolted to the air mattress. My heart raced, my head spun.

This time, lying down didn't help. There I was, alone on the floor, thinking: *What if this isn't Afib, but that stroke I'm so at risk of having?* I stood up unsteadily and called Jean who was at work a block away. I told her I had to come over to her clinic. She told me to go to emerg instead. Somehow I made it downstairs and out onto Bay Street where a friend saw me clinging to a lamppost as I yelled for a cab. I didn't want to call 9-1-1 because the ambulance might take too long. Besides, what if I was taken to the wrong hospital?

At Toronto General, the routine was pretty much like my first visit, and I was discharged that night. Two weeks later, it happened again.

Over the course of the month between my first Afib attack and my third, I went into a profound physical and psychological free fall. When I wasn't in Afib, I was in terror of it. I stopped taking the subway for fear I'd be trapped underground during an attack. Each morning, I was reduced to mapping out which streets I would walk on. They couldn't be side streets. They had to have lots of people, day and night, and most of all, lots of cabs.

After a while, it became clear that I really couldn't work, so I had to lay off my two staff. This left me alone in the office where I puttered with paperwork. But, frankly, my big daytime activity that June and July was snoozing. I'd bought an air mattress and a blanket and would doze off for an hour each morning and two hours each afternoon.

By this time, I was avoiding even the few client meetings I needed to attend. Not just because I didn't want my clients to call 9-1-1, but because there were two occasions when I was in the middle of a meeting and I simply burst into tears. As one of my clients said years after: "Not great for business development."

So I stopped meeting clients in person as much as I could. But even the phone couldn't shield me. I took calls from friends, and again I couldn't stop weeping, and would hang up.

The fact is, I rarely went to the office anymore. I still did my daily walks. But why do anything that would get my heart rate higher and risk flipping into Afib? So I stayed at home, slept, and ate a lot. I gained twenty pounds, filling the holes left by my anxiety.

I gave up reading books because I couldn't remember what I'd read even as I was reading it. I stuck to magazines and newspapers (I remember getting through the entire front section of the *Globe and Mail* one day before I realized it was yesterday's edition). I would lie in bed and watch half a dozen hour-long episodes of *MI-5* in a row.

Three or four days would go by and there would be no attacks. I would think, *Phew, they're over.* But now, even a mild one brought the same terror-inducing fear as a major attack. Jean thought I should see my cardiologist.

Dr. Ross expressed some surprise that I was on such large doses of metoprolol. I told him I was always tired. What I didn't tell him was that I thought the metoprolol was starting to make me crazy. He suggested I switch to a different kind of beta blocker altogether, one called sotalol. We also talked about what could be done to stop the attacks. It was clear that they were not just running my life, they were ruining it.

He said there were three ways out when it came to stopping Afib. The first was drugs. Well, that clearly wasn't working. The second was cardioversion, where your heart is shocked back into normal rhythm. But cardioversion works on only a third of patients. The same with drugs and the third option, ablation: in that, they'd open up my heart again and ablate, or destroy, the areas of abnormal heart tissue that were causing the heart's electrical system to short-circuit.

The last thing I wanted was another round of open-heart surgery. Besides, you often had to wait three to six months after ablation for your heart to move back into normal rhythm.

I left Dr. Ross's office feeling angry and helpless. That night, when I talked to Jean, she admitted that whenever one medical problem has three solutions, generally none of them is really much good. I told her that if each of these procedures only worked a third of the time, then the odds were against me ever beating Afib. She calmly suggested I was getting ahead of myself.

The next morning, a Friday in early August, I went to the drugstore to have my prescription filled for that new beta blocker. The pharmacist explained how often I had to take the pills and suggested I read the product description he had printed off.

I did. It said: "Sotalol should only be taken in a hospital environment under the direct supervision of a cardiologist."

What was this?

"Side effects include heart attack, stroke, and sudden death."

What the hell? I read it over and over.

By the time I got home, there was only one conclusion I could logically draw: my doctors were trying to kill me.

This wasn't just some angry fantasy. I truly believed I could no longer trust my cardiologist, my family doctor, or even my wife.

The fact that Jean was part of a plot to kill me didn't make me angry, just sad. I wasn't even at a loss to understand how the woman who loved me and married me now wanted me dead. I was simply curious. This startling passivity didn't really concern me; I was resigned to my fate.

Then the phone rang. It was a friend who's a doctor, Elaine Chin, wanting to know if I was well enough to write something for her. Instead, I told her about my new beta blockers and how they would kill me. I didn't tell her about Jean because they were friends and ...

I could hear the worry in her voice. She suggested I go to the drugstore and buy a bottle of Tylenol and read the product description. "It will say pretty much the same thing. They all do because they have to mention every conceivable bad outcome. So, Bob ... take ... the ... sotalol!"

I did, half-convinced I was going to drop dead right there.

That same evening, in another desperate effort to exert some control over my life, I told Jean that I was going to check into a hotel that was just a block from the Toronto General Emergency Department.

Jean carefully asked me why I felt I should move into a hotel. I told her — or rather snapped at her — I never wanted to be more than a hundred yards from the hospital. My barking was one part anger at anyone who was listening, because they couldn't solve my problem, and anger at myself that I was completely unable to help myself.

Over the last few weeks, my Afib attacks had happened more often, with greater force, and lasted longer. My memory had also grown shockingly faulty.

So I painstakingly entered every appointment in my Outlook calendar, checking to make sure I had the right time and date and place — and three times in a single week I turned up for meetings twenty-four hours ahead of time, or at the wrong place.

I tried to cling to my work, but I was way too jumpy for writing anything more than a page at most.

Finally, on August 3, I found myself lying on a gurney waiting to be cardioverted.

Cardioverting is a little like being tasered. Big wire patches are taped onto your chest and back. Then you're zapped with a hundred joules of electricity in the hope that your heart will be converted back into a normal *thub-thub-thub* rhythm.

It's no wonder they put you under. But by this time I would do anything to stop the chaos that had taken over my life.

I awoke from that procedure to find my heart — *thub, thub, thub* — beating normally. A few days later, it was still fine.

But still I felt highly anxious. I couldn't understand why my psyche hadn't returned to normal now that my heart had.

Weeks later, a friend called me one night from Chicago. She asked how I was. I burst into tears. I hung up and sent her a text message saying I was fine, really. Those terrible days of Afib were in the past. I could pick up where I'd left off in recovering from my valve replacement.

And I did that; I started to walk to work. I was even willing to walk down side streets. I took the subway. I noticed that I could walk up more stairs without getting out of breath. I actually started to ride my bike.

Then one night after dinner, Jean and I went for a walk. Jean idly mentioned that most of the twelve doctors in her office had had a meeting that afternoon. "Oh, what was that about?" I asked.

"It was about you."

"Me? Really?"

"Yes. It took us ten seconds to determine that you're depressed and then fifteen minutes to figure out what antidepressant you should go on."

I was enraged.

I stopped and turned to her, practically yelling. "I'm not depressed. I'm just sad!"

"Right, darling … So the antidepressant is a tetracyclic and it's called Remeron. Here's the prescription. You can get it filled in the morning."

After my flash of anger, I suddenly felt relieved. Someone cared! The cavalry was coming! But could I really be depressed? It seems I'd forgotten the warning before my operation that one in three patients who has open-heart surgery will suffer from depression.

It takes a few weeks for any antidepressant to kick in, and often weeks longer to fiddle with just the right dosage. But I have to tell you, the very next morning, after I picked up my prescription, taking care not to read the product description, I took my first dose of Remeron and felt better within thirty seconds. As Jean said, so great was my need to feel in control that the placebo effect sped me on my way.

Looking back, it took almost a year after my heart surgery to truly feel myself again. First, there were the three months recovering from the surgery itself. Then three more months of Afib attacks, then six months of depression before I was finally able to marvel at all the things I'd taken for granted before.

I was amazed that the doctors at the Peter Munk Cardiac Centre were right: I *could* run after I got my new valve. It was twice a week at a plodding pace. And I went farther the next day than I did the day before, and that counts for something, too.

But most of all, I marvelled at my heart and the new life it gave me. I wrote a note to myself on the first anniversary of my surgery. I was back to work, writing speeches, hosting speakers, and gathering up friends for concerts and trips.

I didn't cry any more, at least not out of the blue in someone's office. My clients had returned and I could hire a staff again. And once more Jean and I started to travel far and wide.

Today I still marvel that our hearts sit quietly in our chests, beating a hundred thousand times a day in virtually all of the seven billion of us who walk the earth, with only a few of us giving it a second's thought.

Maybe that's why heart disease doesn't get the fear and loathing that cancer does, even though it will kill almost as many of us.

But the greatest marvel for me was that I finally realized I'd been living my life for years as if each day were my last. You can't do that for so long and not develop an extreme lifestyle.

I'd like to say I'm now happiest when I'm doing incredibly ordinary things, like having dinner with Jean, or reading a book, or going for a walk, consciously putting one foot in front of the other. And sometimes I am. Waiting in line used to drive me around the bend. Now it just drives me to frantically search my iPhone for new ways to distract myself.

18   A Bad Role Model

For the past twenty years, I've taught companies how to write more clearly and present more persuasively. I often do this via half-day and one-day courses for a dozen or more executives. These are intense, hard work, for the participants and for me. I have to be "on" all the time and talking much of the time. So it's tiring mentally and physically. I once taught three consecutive one-day courses in Edmonton and could barely speak by the start of day 3.

Looking back, the heavy sessions seem to also happen on days of great threat or celebration for me. Or both at the same time.

In one twenty-four-hour period in 2015, I left the emerg at Toronto General Hospital at midnight, gorked on a beta blocker to slow my suddenly racing heart.

The next morning, looking like hell and feeling like sludge, I taught a class in persuasion, then headed to Mount Sinai Hospital where I was due for oral surgery.

When the dental nurse asked if I'd been hospitalized any time in the last twelve months, I told her that yes, in fact, just last night in the Toronto General emerg unit for my heart. Her eyes widened and her iPad closed and she said, "I think we should cancel your appointment today, Mr. Ramsay. Why don't you call to reschedule when you're feeling better?" She then practically pushed me out the door. *Yikes, we don't want this guy dying in* our *clinic, on* my *watch.*

This was excellent news from my perspective. It let me go to the seventh floor of the same hospital earlier than I'd expected. Jean was waiting there for our daughter-in-law, Kate, to give birth to her and Jean Paul's first child and our first grandchild: the gorgeous, peerless Riley Grace Marmoreo, who is now seven. As I held this tiny one-hour-old human in my arms, I was struck by the look of pure joy in Jean's eyes and how, despite the usual dysfunction in every family, and the mixed nature of ours, this one would be carrying on for at least one more generation. It was clear, even now, that our entire family would shift its gaze to this newest member and that her arrival would change our dynamics forever. Even I knew that new babies have a way of doing that.

I also marvelled at my own luck. I'd missed the parenting part of life, and tried gamely to find my way as a step-parent. But I was here ready to go at the very start of grandparenting. Ready to do whatever grandparents do, but not quite sure what that entailed. As Jean said, "You missed the wet years, honey." The thought of where I'd been in the last twenty-four hours, close to death and now closer still to life, bounced through my head. I tried hard to make sense of it all, but at this moment every thought was a fleeting one. The only idea that stayed with me was the one I left the hospital with, arm in arm with Jean, who said, "Let's go home, honey. We need some sleep."

This pattern of colliding with life and death right after teaching had emerged with a vengeance in 2004. I was booked to teach a writing session from 9:00 a.m. to 1:00 p.m. A few weeks earlier, I'd won a Courage to Come Back Award from CAMH, the Centre for Addiction and Mental Health. I'd "won" in the addictions category, and that evening I and five other awardees would be feted in front of a thousand people at a downtown hotel.

I hadn't forgotten that the year I got sober, in 1990, I had been a guest at this event, which that year was very small and new, and one of my tablemates had railed against addicts getting awards for anything (except for leaving town, I suspected).

Then the week before this 2004 gala, the man whom I had worshipped when I was just starting my career in Toronto, who had introduced me to cocaine, and who, because my hero-worship of him was total and all-consuming, had nearly killed me, himself died in a men's shelter downtown.

Robert Burns had been everything I wasn't and desperately wanted to be. He was a self-made Brit, a graphic designer who'd emigrated to Canada in the 1960s as part of the British Invasion that saw Toronto change from a bland provincial city into the country's creative capital. Brits poured in by the planeload. With his partner Heather Cooper and his Canadian colleagues, James Donoahue and Allan Fleming (who designed the iconic CN logo), he formed the design studio that became Burns, Cooper, Donoahue, and Fleming.

Their work changed the meaning, worth, and prestige of design in Canada. Robert (never Bob) and his partners were doing stuff so much better, so much faster, so much more creatively, that all we could do was stand aside and gasp. Or hope that his heat generated some light in us. One of their first clients was Roots, then a tiny start-up. Soon, big corporations came knocking; and not just Canadian companies, but global ones. They were that good.

Robert's presentations were astonishing. I remember pitching a government of Ontario account with him when, in the middle of the presentation — there were six of us on our team — he got in an argument with his life and work partner, Heather Cooper.

She was speaking when Robert suddenly held up his hand and said, "No, I'm sorry, Heather, you're wrong about that. It's like this ..." Then Heather fought back. "No, Robert, it's not like that at all ..."

There went the big account, I thought, as I saw the civil servants on the other side of the table reel back at this shocking interruption.

But we won, and when I asked the official why, he said, "Oh, because of that argument Robert Burns had in the middle of your presentation. Anyone who can speak truth to power like that isn't going to be afraid to do great work."

When I asked Robert after the pitch what the hell he thought he was doing, he said, "Oh, the whole thing was staged. We just pretended to disagree."

I felt like Bambi at the deer hunt.

Robert and Heather's parties were impossibly cool. They invited me because I loved their work and turned some of my own clients into theirs. But more so because Robert could be his boastful, charming best in front of me, without much effort. He was good-looking and smart — beautiful women always seemed to be draped around him. Heather didn't seem to mind. They lived in a world with different rules.

One night in 1979 I went to their gorgeous home in midtown Toronto, where Heather's fantastical paintings hung on the walls, for a party to welcome an Italian man they were collaborating with. I didn't catch his name at the time. But he too looked and talked and acted as if he was from a perfect planet whose codes and language were alien to me, and I was desperate to learn. I discovered after the party that I'd carried on a brief, loud, and mindless conversation with Massimo Vignelli, at that time the most famous packaging designer in the world.

I was hooked.

At another party soon after, Robert signalled: "Let's go upstairs. I've got some coke." I'd sniffed it once before and was disappointed. I wanted to "feel something," the way you do when you smoke dope. All I felt was clear-headed. And I talked a lot to the friend who gave it to me. A lot. But was that all coke was about? I was a disappointed, dismissive first-time user. *Maybe it would be different the second time*, I thought, as I sat down on a couch on the second floor balcony with Robert, looking down on the crowd of very hip people below. Robert had invited a third person, a beautiful, sexy woman of thirty, who happened to be a nurse.

"Have you ever shot coke?" Robert asked me.

"Shot cocaine?"

"Yes, shot cocaine." Both Robert and the woman, named Mary, were looking intently at me.

"No. Never."

"You want to try now? Mary's a nurse. She's brought the needles. You'll be fine."

The thought of someone injecting cocaine into my veins scared me to death. No way would I do this.

"Here, let me show you."

Robert took out a small bag of white powder, shook a bit of it onto a spoon he'd conveniently brought with him and poured a few drops of water. As the coke was absorbed, Mary took out a small hypodermic needle and drew the clear liquid in the spoon into the needle. Giving it a quick squirt and an expert tap, she handed Robert a long elastic tube that she'd pulled from her purse. He wrapped it around his upper left arm, squeezed his fist, and let

Mary dab his arm with an alcohol swab, then carefully and very professionally slid the needle into one of his large blue arteries. She then gave him a small cotton ball to press down on the entry point to ensure there was no blood.

I was transfixed.

I also wanted to leave.

Within three seconds, Robert had undone the rubber tube, which fell to the floor. He groaned, clearly in ecstasy. Then he laid his head down on the couch. "Oh … oh … ohh … *God* is that good." After about a minute, he suddenly jumped up and walked around the room. "Wow, wow, wow … What an incredible rush! Ramsay, my head's on fire." Mary smiled joyously.

"Come on, try it."

Well, I did. Of course I did. What defences did I have against such an offer?

Forget everything I knew about character, self-respect, risk, sudden death. They were all washed away in the flood of desire to be like these two beautiful people who had it all together, and who could do *anything* they wanted. I wanted to be like them. I wanted to be them. And hey, Mary was a nurse, for heaven's sake. What could go wrong?

At Robert's funeral thirty-five years later, I gave the eulogy and said, "It's no coincidence that the addiction that grabbed hold of Robert and held on for so long was the addiction so many of us had for Robert himself.

"As with all addictions, it was all great at the beginning. Then it became great sometimes and bad sometimes. And by the end, it was all bad, all dreadful, all the time."

I was speaking from the pulpit of St. James Cathedral before a crowd of two hundred mourners, with the archbishop seated to the left of where I stood. I could see him out of the corner of my eye and, at one point, he glowered at me.

"We were hooked on him the way he was hooked on drugs," I continued. "Our withdrawal from him was tough and painful.

"But I'm not here to damn him, nor to stir up an anger that, for many of us has been largely washed away over the twenty-five years when he was ruining his life, living on the streets."

"Nor am I here to excuse his often dreadful behaviour. But I am here to explain something of what plagued him, and maybe in that, we can all get some peace. Because Robert Burns was a drug addict."

I could tell that last sentence really bothered the archbishop. The convention when you're eulogizing an addict or alcoholic is to say that they had many demons and eventually the demons won out.

There was no way I was going to say that. How could I? I'm a drug addict myself. That euphemistic language only helps people stay addicted and families stay ruined. There's a reason no one stands up at an AA meeting and says, "I'm Bob and I have some demons."

Also, when I looked out onto the crowd, I remembered that many of them had been close friends of Robert in the good days. They had also given him many thousands of dollars in the bad days and my sense was that some of them had come just to be sure this man who had escaped death so often actually was dead — as were their efforts to collect from him.

They were sad, for sure, because he was so damned talented, so devilishly enthusiastic, and so demonically charming. But in a way I'd never seen at a funeral, they were mad, too.

Once a year or so, I would run into him when I was out for a long run on some city street and he would be begging passersby for money. I would always run by, thinking, *That could have been me. There but for the grace of ...* and I would always consciously insert the word *Jean* where *God* usually appears because I don't believe in my God as much as I believe in my wife.

In fact, the last time I saw Robert was one summer's night when Jean and I were walking home from her office at Bay and Bloor. A ragged-looking old man was sitting on the sidewalk peddling watercolours. "Paint your portrait for ten dollars," he'd say to passersby. It was his British accent that made me turn my head. I knew that voice. "Robert?" I asked. I leaned down to get a better look at him. His skin was yellow. He looked like a ghost.

Jean stopped, wondering who I was talking to. Robert said, "This must be Jean." She was confused. "Jean, this is Robert Burns." With great effort, Robert stood up. "How do you do, Jean. I've heard so much about you." Always gallant.

"Very nice to meet you, Robert."

"May I paint your beautiful face?"

"I'm fine, thank you."

"Really?"

"I'm fine."

I quickly found a twenty-dollar bill in my pocket and gave it to him.

"Here, Robert, have this." This was too painful. We had to get out of there.

"But you get two portraits for twenty dollars. Let me paint each of you."

"Really, no, Robert." I looked at Jean. "Honey, we have to go."

"Are you sure?" said Robert, sensing my unease.

"It's fine, Robert. Keep the twenty. We have to go." I took Jean's hand and ... off we walked, not turning back.

I felt craven, embarrassed, awful.

"He's got hepatitis," said Jean.

"How do you know?"

"His skin's yellow. He doesn't have long. But the tracks on his arms look old. So he may not be using."

I'd missed all that.

But she was right on both counts. I'd heard that he was finally off drugs, at least for a few months at a time. He was living in a men's shelter run by the Anglican Church and was designing a campaign to help raise funds for men's shelters throughout the city. Of course he was. I had to hand it to him, Robert was irrepressible.

Six months later, I got a phone call from a man who asked me my name and if I knew Robert Burns. He was very sorry to tell me that Robert had died a couple of days ago in the men's shelter at St. James Cathedral. He was cooking dinner for the men and suddenly keeled over and that was that. The caller was wondering if I could let some of his other old friends know because I was the only link he had to Robert's past.

"How did you know to call me?"

"He had your name in his wallet."

"He did?"

I was shocked.

"Just my name?"

"No, there were about ten names on the list, along with phone numbers. His business partners. His daughter. His first wife. People like that.

I thought to myself: *Robert had two wives?*

"Could I ask you to help in another way?"

"Of course."

"We need eight men to be pallbearers at his funeral. It's in a couple of days.

"I'm not sure I can round up eight men who knew him. Aside from the guys in the shelter, though they likely won't make it to the funeral."

"When's the funeral, again?"

"Wednesday at one o'clock at St. James Cathedral on King Street."

I could make it. I'd have to bike like hell from my presentation training session that ended at twelve thirty. And then I'd have to leave right after for the 2:00 p.m. rehearsal for the Courage to Come Back dinner that night.

"Who's speaking at the funeral?"

"We're not sure. Maybe you can suggest some names for that, too."

"Me. I want to speak."

"Did you know him well?"

He meant it curiously, not aggressively. But I had to be sure.

"Very well. I'm going to speak."

He was slightly taken aback.

"Sure. Fine. We'll put you on the list."

"Who else is speaking?"

"Well, as I said, we're just starting to put together the list, and … if you know anyone else from his past …"

"I'll give the eulogy. I want to give the eulogy."

"Well, it's in the cathedral and the archbishop says he'll be there, so he'll lead the service."

"Fine. He can do that. I'll give the eulogy … and I'll also try to find some pallbearers."

I hung up and wondered what had come over me, that I was so insistent I speak.

Part of me wanted to make sure the world saw that I was not him, though anyone with eyes could see I was so like him. We were an odd couple. He was my mentor, for better and for much *much* worse. I also demanded the podium to show that I chose to live and he didn't. I stopped taking drugs and he didn't. But in life as in new death, we were still a couple of outsiders competing to be accepted.

The morning of the funeral I gave the shortest wrap-up of any class I'd ever taught. Then I got on my bike and pedalled like a lunatic the six miles to the cathedral. I made it with fifteen minutes to spare, still pouring sweat from the ride.

The man who phoned to tell me of Robert's death came up to me, panic-stricken. They only had five men to carry the coffin, including me. Did I know anyone walking in to the funeral I could ask to be a pallbearer?

It had come to this. I buttonholed an old mutual friend of Robert's I knew and said, "David, you need to do me and Robert a favour." He said yes, but not before looking at me as if this was another Robert Burns scam. Which is likely why he said, "He's dead, right? He's in the coffin?"

"Yes, yes to both."

By the time the service began, we had our eight pallbearers. When it ended, we walked to the coffin, which was close to the altar, lifted it up from the wheeled cart it had come in on and carried it awkwardly out to the front of the church onto King Street, where a hearse was waiting. With the help of the funeral home staff, we slid the coffin into the hearse and the other pallbearers all turned to go back into the church where the crowd was still milling about and reminiscing about Robert.

I turned the other way, got on my bike, and rode to the Harbour Castle hotel, where the rehearsal for the Courage to Come Back awardees was just beginning.

The idea that I'd be late for my own funeral crossed my mind, but I quickly dismissed it. The day was steaming with symbols — and it would produce many more.

At the hotel, I was immediately taken by the organizers to a green room, where I met my fellow "winners." We congratulated each other on overcoming everything from schizophrenia to the urge to commit suicide. I did get the sense that the others thought I was a bit of an interloper, since I was "just" an addict. But I thought it best not to mention the funeral I'd just come from. It would take too long to explain that addiction, like depression and many other brain disorders, is a disease, like cancer and heart disease.

Each awardee sat at a table sponsored by one of CAMH's supporters. We got to invite our significant other and three friends, which for me were Charles Fremes and his wife, Judith McDermid, and Bernita Drenth, the widow of Arthur Gelgoot, who, along with Charles, had intervened on me fourteen years earlier.

The evening itself is a blur. Lots of handshaking and backslapping, and of course a speech.

After the ball was over, Charles and Judith drove us all home in their car. Home for Jean that night was the delivery suite of Women's College Hospital, where she was on call every Wednesday overnight. By this stage in her career, she'd pulled so many all-nighters for so long that I literally couldn't tell the next day if she'd had eight hours sleep, or none.

Doctors have done this for centuries, which tells me simply that you can train yourself to make anything normal. But if I got zero hours of sleep one night, I'd barely function — as anyone looking at me would see.

Charles and Judith then dropped me at our condo at Pape and Danforth, and, no surprise, it was impossible to get to sleep. I was high from my speech at the CAMH Awards, higher still from all the adulation around my "courage" — though there was not one single second in the fourteen years of my staying clean and sober that I'd thought I exhibited "courage." Doggedness, sure. A terrifying fear of relapsing, which is likely why I demonized my addiction so much. One small slip and I would never come back.

But that fear was nothing compared to the one about Jean walking out of my life if I let drugs back in. She'd made it very clear in the week I got back from Atlanta that that was the deal. And as we'd built our lives together over those fourteen years since, a life that put our old lives more in the shadow with every passing day, the idea of throwing this all away was just too frightening for me to bear.

I hadn't even turned my head to what the first part of this astounding day meant. Robert Burns's funeral, both on its own and as context to the dinner that followed, would keep me awake for many hours that night. The only solution, the only way I could close my eyes long enough to function the next day was … warm milk!

Yes, that would do it. I would go downstairs, heat up some milk, and drift off to sleep.

Warm milk. This is what my life had come to.

The next morning, I was up and out the door on my bike to the office. My glorious mood was heightened by the hot sun and the cloudless sky. At eight o'clock, my mobile phone rang. I pulled over to the curb on Queen Street to answer it. I could see it was a friend of mine who was a patient of Jean's. She had a big job in the Ontario Government.

"Hi, Jan. What's up?"

"Where's Jean?"

Not "Good morning, Bob, could I speak with your wife?"

I'd had these urgent "I need her now" calls before.

"She's at the hospital."

I heard her yelling at her two young kids to sit down on the couch. Now!

Odd. She never spoke like that. I wondered where her husband was — Tim was a long-standing friend of mine and an even bigger power player than his wife.

"Where's Tim?"

"He's in the kitchen. He told us over breakfast that he loves us all but that he wants to take his life. He's just sitting there. The kids are in tears."

"What?!"

"Yes, and I need Jean to tell me what to do."

"Hold on, Jan. Let me try to get her. Don't hang up."

I quickly dialed Jean, praying that she wasn't delivering a baby or somewhere her phone wasn't. She was terrible about letting the battery run down, or simply leaving her phone at home when she went on call.

She picked it up on the first ring. "Good morning," she said cheerily. "And how —"

"Jean, Jan Colville's on the other line." I spat out the story as fast as I could.

"Put her on," was all Jean said.

Jean and I listened to her. Then Jean interjected …

"Has he gone to the bathroom?" she asked.

"No."

"Don't let him. At least don't let him close the door. Don't let him out of your sight. Even now. Can you see him?"

"Yes. Yes, I can."

"Good. Then call a cab and when it gets there, put all four of you into it. If the cabbie objects, give him twenty bucks.

"Have him take you to the CAMH Emergency Unit on Russell Street. Not CAMH on Queen Street.

"Take the elevator to the admitting desk on the ground floor.

"Tell them who you are, show them your business card.

"Tell them politely you want to speak with the psychiatrist-on-call. When he comes out, don't leave. Stay there until you see him take Tim through the unit door and you hear the lock click shut.

"Then call me."

Jan did all that. Tim didn't commit suicide, though he was pretty sick for a long time.

And as I rode my bike to work and thought back on the previous twenty-four hours — on Robert Burns's funeral, on the Courage to Come Back Awards, and on Jean's intervention of a suicide-in-the-making, the only thought that stayed in my mind was, I am one very lucky man.

19 Running for Women, and for Cover

I t was less than a bang and more than a whimper.

I was standing in a crowd two blocks from the finish line of the Boston Marathon on April 15, 2013, when we all heard a muffled *boom*.

Thousands of us lined Stuart Street in the Family Meeting Area, waiting in strict alphabetical order for our loved ones who'd just finished the race to meet us under the first letter of our last names. I always waited for Jean, not under the *M* taped to a telephone pole, but under the *A* on another. It was the closest pole to the corrals whose chutes every finisher walked through, picking up their gear, food, and drink after running 26.2 miles from Hopkinton, Massachusetts, into downtown Boston to cross the finish line of the most famous marathon in the world.

What sets Boston apart from London, or Berlin, or New York, or any of the hundreds of other marathons is that you have to qualify even to get to the start line. Every age group has a different qualifying time, and only certain other marathons are qualifying runs. Hence, Boston's reputation for toughness and purity. Boston is also one of the oldest marathons on earth. First run in 1897, it's held on the third Monday in April, which is Patriot's Day, a civic holiday. The bars open at 9:00 a.m. and the crowds on the street are huge. It's America the Boisterous celebrating their city with some of the top athletes in the world.

This was Jean's sixth Boston Marathon and the fourth where she finished first among women in her age group. A few minutes earlier, I could see from the Boston Marathon app on my phone that she'd done it again, and I waited with a big smile to greet her as she searched for me in the *As* on Stuart Street.

I was surrounded by families and runners in the happy chaos that bubbles up at the end of every marathon. Runners limping, relatives crying, high-fiving teams who'd raised thousands of dollars for their favourite causes; all the joy that flows from doing something so hard after training thousands of hours to join thirty thousand others at the start line. Do that on a sunny day and your faith in humankind is overflowing. Do it in Boston and the feeling is sublime.

That's one of the things that hooked us on marathons. They're gigantic celebrations of so much that's worthwhile in the world. In numbers your fellow travellers are bigger than a small city and your cheerleaders can measure in the millions. Talk about being larger than life and close to your fellow humans.

It was this hugeness that instantly drew me to the photo Cathy Orcutt showed us in the summer of our wedding, and which had spurred us to run the New York City Marathon the next year. That was our first marathon, and it had been life-changing.

However, by 2001 our marathon careers were at an end. I had a sore back, which made running painful and caused me to drop out of the San Antonio Marathon five miles in. Jean was writing her book about midlife women and their health. Her idea for *The New Middle Ages* was that midlife for North American women, which used to be a waiting room, was now a supermarket. Their menopause symptoms could be managed and their day-to-day lives could mean more and be happier. For the past year Jean had been writing a weekly column in the *Globe and Mail.* These were basically tales from the examining room, and she fought constantly to tell her patients' stories while respecting their confidentiality. Those 750 words every week were almost as hard to disguise as to write. So the prospect of writing a seventy-five-thousand-word book, which would be published the next spring, was daunting.

But getting it written, and being a full-time doctor, and training for a marathon? One of them had to give, and so we decided that we'd make our last race the Marine Corps Marathon in Washington, D.C., in October 2001.

And from this was born JeansMarines, the women's marathon group that ran through Washington for seven glorious, gnawing years, whose members still hit the streets of Toronto today and whose story is told in chapter 15.

When JeansMarines stopped running in 2008, Jean just kept going. Tired of coaching the slowest JeansMarines, she wanted to go faster. She ran for the first time in Boston in 2009 and still runs it — and only it — today.

But back to April 15, 2013.

It was a gorgeous day when Jean made her way past the finish line on Boylston Street through the chutes, picking up her shiny thermal blanket, a banana, and Gatorade. She craved the salty chicken sandwich I had waiting for her under the *A* in the Family Meeting Area two blocks away. It was slow-going as it always is at a marathon finish line as runners suddenly pull up and stop. It's hard to move forward in the big crowd ahead of you, and with people piling in behind you, impossible to move back. While it can often take a good half-hour after you finish to get to the Meeting Area, on this day, it only took her ten minutes. She was almost at the family meeting area when she heard a muffled *boom* behind her. Fireworks? People were yelling as she was pushed forward. The runners looked at each other, confused. Then sirens. Lots and lots of sirens. She learned later that the police pushed the runners who'd finished to get them away from the finish line.

As for the hundreds of us waiting under the *A* for our runners, it was just as chaotic. Because there was a building between us and the finish line blocking the view and muffling the sound, no one was sure if the sound was an explosion or not. We tried to use our cellphones, but they didn't work. We learned later that the police had shut down all cellular service in the area for fear that the bombs were activated by cellphones.

While we'd done this "meet up at the *A* sign" many times, for half an hour it seems Jean was looking for me and I was looking for her, and we didn't see each other. So I left my post at *A* and headed to the finish line two blocks away to search for her. It took me nearly an hour to get back.

It was now getting cold in the late afternoon. What to do? I had to move, had to do something. I got out three business cards, found some tape, and stuck them on the telephone pole, hoping Jean would see the big orange *Ramsay* and the word *hotel* etched with my key into the top card. I reasoned that if she hadn't made it out of the corral by now, and I could see that it was deserted, she was either in a First Aid tent or at a hospital. So I started walking. But it soon became clear that no one except first responders was allowed anywhere near the finish line. I then turned around and made my way to the First Aid tent in the corral. I walked in. I expected to see high security and broken bodies. But it was deserted inside. No runners, no paramedics. Nobody.

Meanwhile, Jean had been waiting at *A* for half an hour and started to chill down, to the bone. So she began walking back to the hotel, hoping her "space blanket" would keep her warm enough for the long walk. She remembers sitting in Boston Common by the lake watching a mom with her toddler feeding the ducks, while sirens rang on all the roads surrounding the park. Our flight home wasn't far off and she was damned if she was going to get on the plane without having a shower. So she kept walking back to the hotel.

I called the hotel, praying my phone worked again. It did. I got through to the concierge. Was my wife there? No, she wasn't in the room. Please, please, leave a message for her!

By the time she got to the hotel, the concierge rushed up to her and said, "Oh, Mrs. Ramsay, your husband is looking for you." But it was only when she got into the room and saw the TV, which we'd left on when we left much earlier that day, that she truly understood what she'd escaped. Not one bomb, but two. She dived into the shower, fast.

Meanwhile, I can't tell you the utter panic I felt. No Jean. No way to reach her. I was all alone. But I had to keep moving or I would disintegrate.

It was a good two miles to the hotel. There were no cabs, only ambulances and police cars. As I made my way through Boston Common, I tried calling Jean. This time the phone rang but I knew she'd left her phone in the room, so I left a message to say I'd meet her there.

In the half hour it took me to get to our hotel on the waterfront, I had plenty of time to catastrophize about Jean's death and my life afterward. We used to say to our accountant that she should treat us as a single economic unit. But in the twenty years of our marriage, we had grown to be a single emotional and intellectual unit, as well. If we didn't finish each other's sentences, it was because we'd both moved on to the next subject. Life was so gigantically better from when we'd first met that I couldn't imagine it going back to that unhappy state without her. I wouldn't be able to go on without her. I would take cocaine, but only to end my life.

My reverie was punctuated by some very real practicalities. Who should I call after I told the kids their mother was dead? How would I get her body back to Toronto? Who would speak at the funeral?

As I reached the hotel, I saw a group of runners milling inside the lobby. I went through the door, and a young woman came out from behind the front desk and asked, "Are you Mr. Ramsay?"

"Yes." I knew it. Jean was dead.

"Your wife asked me to tell you she's upstairs in the room."

I burst into tears.

"Really!" I ran for the elevator.

I opened the door to our room. "Jean?"

"Jean!"

No one was there.

"Jean!"

The bathroom door opened and she came out in a bathrobe, steam rising from the shower she'd just finished. We hugged and kissed like mad. Oh god. Oh god. Oh god.

"Where were you!" I was almost yelling.

"The crowd was so tight, I couldn't get out of the corral. I finally got to the *A*s and no one was there. Then I spotted your business card and I did what I was told, my dear. I came back to the hotel."

It was four thirty. Our flight home was at eight.

"Are you hungry?"

"I'm famished."

"Well, here's your chicken sandwich."

It had gotten cold in my jacket pocket, and was bent and soggy by the time I pulled it out. But she ate it ravenously — starved for salt.

"Our flight's at eight. Let's turn on the TV and see what happened."

"Honey, I just want to get out of town. Why don't we go to the airport and maybe we can catch the six o'clock flight."

Jean dressed and we packed up, checked out, and grabbed a cab to the airport.

Halfway to Logan, my phone rang. It was Dan O'Connor, the retired Marine major who had become our friend-in-chief with JeansMarines.

He was working in intelligence for Homeland Security and was on a course at the Naval Postgraduate School in California. We'd spoken earlier in the day; he always double-checked Jean's finish time in case my app didn't pick it up.

"Where are you?" he said.

"In a cab on our way to the airport."

"They're going to shut down the airport in half an hour."

How did he know that? Right. Of course he would know that.

"You're lucky you left the hotel when you did."

"Really? Why?"

"Because they've put the entire downtown Boston in lock-down."

"What does that mean?"

"It means if you're inside your hotel, you can't leave. And if you're outside your hotel, you can't get in."

"If you want to get home," Dan said, "rent a car at the airport and head west on the Mass Turnpike."

Which is exactly what we did, from a booth at the airport half an hour before they shut the place down.

This was the second time I'd lied on a rental form about how long I'd have the car and where I'd drop it off. The first was on 9/11 when I rented a car in New York, said I'd be returning it there in four days, then headed straight home to Toronto. Because you can't rent a car in the U.S. and drop it off in Canada, and vice versa.

But I didn't care. I'd have that fight back in Toronto.

So we headed west into the sunset, with National Guard convoys headed east into Boston on the Turnpike. We turned on the car radio, and three hours after the bombing we finally learned what had happened at the finish line. Jean propped her feet on the dashboard. She'd just run 26.2 miles, then walked two miles more. But she was higher than a kite.

When Jean called the kids, Lara answered — in tears.

"Mom, we thought you were dead!"

Lara had called me, but couldn't get through because my voice mail was full, something that never happens. I'd turned off my phone to save the battery. When I turned it back on there were twenty messages, from family, friends, and the media. They knew Jean was running and they needed a Canadian angle on the Boston Marathon Bombing that was now the top news item all over the world.

As we were driving Jean got an email from a patient, a night editor at the *Globe and Mail*. She asked if Jean could write something about her experience that day. And if she would get it in before 10:00 p.m., so much the better.

Jean turned to me and said, "Let's do it."

She pulled out her laptop from the back seat and started writing. She'd write a paragraph then read it aloud to me. I'd say, "No, no, you have to change that."

We'd argue back and forth about what to say and how to say it better, my hands on the wheel, hers on her laptop.

And the two of us spent the next hundred miles headed home writing and editing and cobbling her piece together before pulling in to a roadside restaurant to email it to the *Globe*.

Here's some of what it said:

> It was hard to talk to our family when we phoned them. The tears came as a release — from the effort spent, from gratitude and luck, from the love of loved ones, from relief.
>
> Bob had been in New York on 9/11.
>
> I remember how panicked I had been about his safety.
>
> I remember he had rented one of the last cars in Manhattan and driven home the next morning, leaving at dawn and driving out across the George Washington Bridge as the Army units and doctors drove in.
>
> We knew then that our world had changed and safety could and never would be assured for any of us again. But somehow until yesterday, we believed that this celebration of determination, this manifesto of pride and grit called the Boston Marathon would elude this horrific inevitability.
>
> Will I run Boston next year?
>
> Well, when we first took our group of 75 Toronto women under the banner of JeansMarines to run the Marine Corps Marathon in Washington, it was just days after the sniper attack in October 2002.
>
> Many of us and our families were afraid to go. But it was [former Toronto mayor] Barbara Hall who wrote us all days before to say: "We have

unfinished business to attend to, and we will not
be stopped by a man with a gun."

So yes, of course I'll run Boston next year, as
should we all.

Around midnight, we checked in to a motel off the highway, still
headed north to the Canadian border at Gananoque.

We turned on the TV and it was only then that we saw the car-
nage the radio couldn't convey.

Ten minutes, I thought. *She finished ten minutes before the bombs
exploded. She was in the race over four hours, and she finished ten minutes ahead of the bombs.*

Just before we got to the border the next morning, Jean put her
finisher's medal around her neck.

The Canada Border Services officer saw it and congratulated her.
She saw the Massachusetts licence plates and asked to see my rental
contract.

"You know you can't bring a rented U.S. car into Canada."

"Yes, I do. But this was the only way we could get home."

She looked at me, looked at Jean, and said, "Okay, but be sure to
return it straight to the rental company when you get to Toronto."

How Canadian.

"We will, for sure."

And on we drove to Toronto. We did turn the car in right away,
then headed with our bags to Jean's clinic, where she was already
half a day late to see her patients. When we arrived in the office, the
medical secretaries all burst into tears.

Soon a small crowd of patients and doctors made their way
to the front area. Nandini Sathi, one of Jean's medical colleagues,
spoke for everyone when she asked, "What's the most dangerous
place in the world?

"Wherever Jean and Bob are standing."

20 Is "The Big C" Cocaine or Cancer?

In September of 2014 Jean and I were bicycling through the hills of Virginia horse country. Pedalling with us were 2,500 other bicyclists on a "Backroads Century," one of the many hundred-mile (or in Canada, hundred-kilometre) one-day bike rallies held each fall in scenic venues across America. We'd taken up Centuries as a way for Jean to cross-train for her marathons and for me to stay in shape by bicycling more than to and from work. This wasn't a race, but a rally. So we took our time at the food and drink stops along the way. At one of them, about forty-six miles into the day, I stepped into a portaloo to pee.

I looked down into the urinal. The liquid hitting the rim wasn't clear or even yellow. It was red. Deep, dark red.

I was peeing blood.

My first thought wasn't, *Oh god, what's this?!* It was, *Why isn't this hurting?* It felt perfectly normal, which gave my denial an opening. *It can't be serious. I'm not in pain.* As I continued to pee, I felt as if I was passing something else through my penis than pee. Again, it didn't hurt, but when it popped out, it was half an inch in diameter and was neither liquid nor solid. It was gross and alien and that's when I got scared. Were my intestines falling out?

I zipped myself up, left the portaloo and walked out to Jean who was waiting on her bike.

"Honey, I just peed blood."

"Really? How dark was it?"

"Very dark. Almost black."

"Any pain?"

"No."

"Any clots?" I guess that was the thing that popped out.

"Ya, I think so."

"Okay, well, if you're feeling okay, get back on your bike and we'll finish the day and then let's see what it is."

The next time I peed, at the finish line, the blood was a little less black. The time after that time, in the airport on the way home, a little less still, and by the time we flew home that night, my pee was a kind of medium red. And no more clots.

By the next day, I was fine.

"What was it?"

Jean told my doctor, Rae Lake, who was also her medical partner and our cottage neighbour. Rae said he'd had another patient the same thing happened to: he'd finished a long-distance bike race on his racing bike, with its narrow seat jammed high into his crotch, just like mine was. Rae also noted that I'm on blood thinners because of my heart. So I bleed and bruise easily.

That was likely what happened, a diagnosis reinforced over the next weeks when my urine was clear even after I got off my bike from three- and six-mile rides. Not to worry.

Later that fall, Jean and I were hiking with six friends in the mountains of Bhutan — the first part of a holiday that would also take us bicycling through the mountains of Laos.

I peeled off from the group to find a bush to pee behind and ... uh-oh ... there it was again: deep, rich, red with clots, lots of clots. I caught up to Jean and told her. That afternoon in our tent she said we'd have to fly home when our Bhutan trip was done in three days and cancel our biking in Laos. Something was up and I needed to be tested. Soon.

We arrived back in Toronto early in the afternoon and three hours later I was getting an ultrasound at Women's College Hospital, which Jean had arranged from Bhutan. The doctor, a tall, middle-aged woman who knew Jean, introduced herself when I checked in and turned me over to the technician who would do the test.

Technicians and doctors are trained not to reveal anything when they're doing a test that might communicate bad news. Let's get the results in and then worry, or not.

But this technician, a Filipino man who'd been doing ultrasounds for years at Women's, well, he looked *very* concerned after he passed the device over my abdomen, and especially when he went back and forth, over and over, on the same spot.

When he finished, he said I should go to the waiting room and the doctor would talk to me about the results. I waited twenty minutes and the doctor came out. She was a different person: she barely looked at me, didn't smile, and said curtly, "We'll send your results to Dr. Lake. He'll talk to you about the results."

Now I was scared. I got home and told Jean about the technician and his curt colleague. She said not to worry and we could both meet Rae Lake the next day in their office.

The next morning, Jean called from her office and told me that I had a CT scan scheduled at noon at Women's College.

"Really? What's wrong?"

"Well, the ultrasound picked up something, but we're not quite sure. The CT will find out."

After I did the CT, the technician said she'd send the results to my doctor the next day and I could talk to him.

But that evening, after dinner, Jean sat me down and said, "So let me tell you about your tests."

"You know about my tests?"

"Well, the ultrasound did actually pinpoint something and it looked to be a tumour in either your pancreas or your prostate. I didn't want to tell you because you'd be up all night with worry."

She had that right.

Pancreatic cancer? Isn't that the worst, most deadly cancer of all? And prostate cancer? That's what my father died of.

This time, no denial could keep my mind from spinning. I was gripped with fear. This was it. The fatal diagnosis, which at some level I'd been waiting for all my life, had arrived, and been delivered by my wife.

"Oh, Christ."

"Honey, honey, let me finish."

"Finish?! I'm finished for Christ's sake!"

"No, you're not. But the ultrasound is why you had the CT so quickly. And I got the results this afternoon."

"How'd you do that?"

"I went to the hospital and found them online. I have them here."

She pulled a long strip of paper from her bag with images of my abdomen sliced neatly into many parts, which is the CT's job — to provide a three-dimensional, multi-angled image of a part of your body.

She could just as well be showing me images of pharaonic Sanskrit.

"The CT clearly shows that there is a tumour. But it's not in your pancreas or your prostate. It's in your bladder. It looks like you have bladder cancer."

Many people — millions today and billions throughout history — have heard news like this. For some, it's clear, understood, and easily absorbed. Not for me. I just sat there, mute. I couldn't even say my brain was spinning. It had stopped. I had to unpack and process what I'd just heard.

First, I had cancer.

Second, it could have been pancreatic cancer (a certain, swift death), or prostate cancer (an uncertain, slow death). But it was neither. It was a cancer I'd never paid much attention to. But I guess when you start peeing blood, that's a pretty good indicator for bladder cancer.

"Bladder cancer?" I didn't even know what that meant.

"Honey, it's good news." (Jean would never say "great news.")

"Why?"

"Because if you've got to have cancer, bladder cancer is the one to have."

"Why is that?"

"Well, it's treatable, and it looks from the CT as if the tumour's small. The surgeon will find that out, though, when he goes in. It seems your blood thinner may have saved your life. You started to bleed early."

"Surgeon?"

"I've already talked with Sidney Radomski at Toronto Western. You're to call his office in the morning and book an appointment. He'll advise you, but the next step is likely going to be surgery. Here's his number."

With that, Jean gave me a quick hug, told me it was going to be okay, and started to make dinner.

I once said you don't get any points in our household for lying around on the couch feeling sorry for yourself. Jean had made it clear that there's absolutely no reason to feel sorry or feel anything but relieved. After all, she's the one who held in her head all the night before (and kept from me) the potentially fatal news from my ultrasound.

Her manner just then also kept me from falling apart. I wondered later why she hadn't tossed and turned all night.

But my first impulse was to *do* something … to move … to think … to get out of the house.

"I'll be back in a bit. I'm just going to the store."

This is a five-minute walk I've done hundreds of times. To the Foodland on Danforth to get dinner, and back. In the first week of recovering from my heart surgery in 2011, it was all I could do to walk painfully slowly the hundred yards up to Danforth and back. Gradually, I was able to make it a hundred yards more to the Foodland, and home. At this moment, I felt exactly the same.

I felt I was the victim of that joke that begins: "I've got good news and bad news."

I had cancer and needed surgery (bad news).

It wasn't pancreatic cancer (good news).

I thought back to when my sister told me in 1971 I had a second sister. I didn't feel anything.

Or when I read my First Step aloud to my fellow patients in the drug treatment centre in 1990 and was told it was the Worst First Step Ever and I wouldn't be leaving any time soon. Again, not a whiff of fear or dread came over me.

Or in 2011 when Jean told me I'd died. I was curious about how it happened, to be sure, but somehow removed from even thinking about it.

I know now that my denial is so entrenched as a survival skill it instantly puts a pillow over any feeling that tries to leap up and shake me.

I write about My Denial as if it's an object, something removed from me, when of course it's not only part of me, it drives a great deal of my psyche completely.

My memory? Never great and now, at age sixty-nine, skipping across the record like a dull needle. But when it comes to awkward encounters with myself, my denial has always kept them safely out of memory's reach. Forgetting is denial's best friend.

But while denial keeps us all from looking back, it also keeps me from thinking forward. In times of turmoil, it's hard for anyone to think straight. But I've found it almost impossible. Even if I hector myself: *I* must *think what this cancer means.*

Ten seconds later, I've skittered on to something else ... the old Greek lady dressed in black passing me on the Danforth, the sign in the bank window reading, "You're richer than you think," the flowers outside Foodland that send me straight to when I was a teen delivering arrangements of them to hospitals and funeral homes as a driver for Walter Ramsay Florists in Edmonton.

So the next few weeks are a blur. I had no plan and thought often of John Lennon's line about just when you're making other plans, life steps in and ... poof.

I did manage to think I shouldn't worry about planning anything until my surgery was over. We all know the anti-planning protocol around cancer because our parents and friends have been down this path. Some go so deep so fast they never return. Others go down one floor and soon pop back up to ground — only to find months or years later the doors never really opened and they're on their way down for good. But more and more these days, still others prove that cancer is a disease you live with, not die from.

I made my way back from Foodland with some fresh tulips in hand and gave them to Jean. She knew why I so needed to take that walk. She also knew as a doctor, as my wife, and from herself, that fifteen minutes after hearing the shocking news is when patients and people and especially her husband would have absorbed it and be able to talk about it.

I wasn't quite ready. I had to go through another ritual first. "So how long do I have to live?"

"About as long as you did before you started peeing blood."

"For sure?" I was insisting that she guarantee the cancer diagnosed in me just one day before would have absolutely no effect on me.

"No, of course not for sure, dear." She looked hard into my eyes. "I'm just saying that this is something we'll get through and when we know more, we'll be able to plan."

My surgery was scheduled for early in December. I turned up at Toronto Western Hospital a few weeks before to chat with Dr. Sidney Radomski. The last thing you expect a urologist to be is funny. But to start with, his licence plate reads LEAKS.

I googled him, of course. I wanted to make sure my bladder was in the hands of someone who knew what he was cutting. Everyone who goes through major surgery does this, of course.

We all want an edge, and if my surgeon is also a professor and a fellow and publishes peer-reviewed research in journals whose names I know, I know the surgery will be a success. That's not true, of course. One of the best cardiac surgeons in the country replaced my aortic valve four years earlier, and the next day I died. It wasn't his fault, of course. I'm just saying there are no guarantees.

But having roomed with half a dozen alcoholic and drug-addicted doctors when I was in treatment in 1990, I've learned not to trust appearances, especially with my life. One of my roommates told me how to pick a surgeon: never go for the most famous or bejewelled. Take the rising star instead. Apparently, a famous singer insisted that the chair of the department take out some nodes in her throat. He botched the operation because he was old and distracted and not up on the latest techniques. She never sang onstage again.

I thought of that when I saw Radomski, then googled him again and found he was in his early fifties. Right in between.

In the two months between my diagnosis and my surgery, we told only our family.

After my year of living dangerously in 2011 around my heart and having to lay off my two staff because I couldn't work to bring in enough money to pay for anyone but me, I didn't need another financial setback. I could hear them whispering, "That Bob Ramsay sure does get sick a lot."

It turns out that my surgery was on a Thursday morning, and if all went well, they'd keep me overnight and send me home Friday morning. I should be able to pee after surgery, though there would likely be bleeding. But it turned out I couldn't pee after I woke up from the anaesthetic. I'd squeeze and squeeze and couldn't get a drop out. Meanwhile, my bladder was bursting.

I had a faint memory of why the Haudenosaunee needed to sew up only one orifice of the Catholic missionaries they tortured before setting them on fire. The nurse quickly fitted me up with a catheter, which delivered blessed relief. They sent me home wearing it — not as uncomfortable as I'd feared, but still weird and clunky.

They also gave me some Percocet in case I had any post-operative pain. I was always watchful around narcotics. As a cocaine addict I could never understand why people got addicted to Percs. It just turned them into slobbering lapdogs, and who wants that when you could be up, Up, UP! instead?

Dr. Radomski came into my room just before I was discharged to say the surgery was a success. By this he didn't mean I was cancer-free. He meant he excised the tumour and found no other tumours. The real result would come a week later from the pathology lab. Then we'd know if it was cancerous and spreading.

Late Friday afternoon Jean came to pick me up and we waited for a cab in the hospital lobby. The pain in my abdomen had been slowly rising, but suddenly it got very sharp. Jean asked if they'd given me any painkillers to take home. Yes, Percocets. "Well, take one," she said, "and let's see how you feel when we get home."

So I fumbled around my coat pocket for the bottle, took it over to the drinking fountain, twisted the cap, and took out … well, took out two Percs and swallowed them down.

I don't like pain. I do like drugs.

By the time the cab had driven us the six miles home, I was that slobbering lapdog. I could barely open the cab door and Jean had to help me walk to our front door. I lay down immediately, unable to move my head for fear I'd be sick. Actually, I was afraid I was going to overdose. No such luck. I fell asleep on the couch for hours.

Despite very clear evidence to the contrary, I somehow thought I'd be up and ready to walk, run, cycle, ski, do anything the next day. Even though I still couldn't pee on my own and was wearing the catheter. I remember feeling the same way before my heart surgery four years earlier. The doctors said it would be six weeks until I got back to work. They clearly didn't know me, how driven and fit I was. I figured four weeks maximum, with time off for good behaviour. I was wrong by about nine months.

Part of this is denial, of course. *If I can just get up, I can't be sick. See?*

But this time, I had a real need to appear to be normal and healthy — and fast. On Sunday, my one-year-old granddaughter,

Riley Grace Marmoreo, was going to be baptized at Metropolitan Community Church by its senior pastor, the Rev. Brent Hawkes.

I was determined to be there. I didn't have kids of my own, so I missed all those precious early age ceremonies. But Riley Grace was my granddaughter and Brent Hawkes was my friend and I'd spoken from the very podium that he'd welcome her from. Oh, and Jean and I had invited two dozen close friends not only to the baptism itself, but to a luncheon afterward at our home. I *had* to be there. There's no way they could *know*.

I woke up with Jean at eight on Sunday morning, exhausted and groggy. I got out of bed wearing my catheter and immediately felt wobbly. Not good. I got up again and this time stayed up. But one thing was clear. There was no way I was going to be able to get dressed in a suit and get down to the car, let alone sit and stand for an hour in a church, then come home and be bright and sparky for another hour, eating and drinking and chattering with a bunch of guests who happened to be close friends.

And do all this wearing a catheter, and without them knowing a thing.

It's amazing how quickly reality can change your view of what's important. Jean has always done this for me. "Well, honey, you stay home and get some more sleep. Then try to join us when we all get back for lunch."

Oh. Sure. Okay.

My fear that my closest friends would all know I was "sick again" simply fell away.

Of course they would. Who was I kidding? And so what if they knew? I had soon come to realize my clients didn't flee because I had heart troubles four years before. They left because I couldn't get the work done. Another strident misperception on my part.

But I was determined to see my granddaughter baptized. This didn't involve my dragging myself onto the street and hailing a cab to the church. All I had to do was log in to the church's website and there it was, live-streamed for anyone to see. I thought of how many times a ceremony like this is performed every Sunday around the world, how many tens of millions of times it's been done over the years, and how important it is.

So I sat up in bed watching the entire service, long after Brent Hawkes had dabbed Riley's face with water, sparking a loud howl from her and great laughs from the congregation.

The food for the party afterward was laid out in the kitchen downstairs and I put on a ratty old bathrobe and went down to nibble on a bit of brunch. The guests would start arriving soon. What would I tell them? I was struck that my first impulse was to make up a story that would make everything seem wonderful. Forced back on reality — I had a catheter tube down my leg, I looked pale, I had cancer, and I had surgery two days ago.

The buzzer rang, signalling the arrival of ... well, exactly who I didn't know, though I knew I knew them well. There was a knock on our door and I went to open it.

"Hi, Bernita!" — one of our great friends and the widow of Arthur Gelgoot, who intervened on me twenty-five years before.

"Bob?" She put her hand to her mouth, her eyes wide. "Where were you?!"

"I had an operation on Thursday. Bladder."

"Are you okay?"

"I think so. They took out a tumour."

"Tumour? Oh Christ."

I repeated a variation of those three words over the entire gathering: "Operation ... Bladder ... Tumour." Our guests started piling in and could figure out the rest.

As the party switched into high gear, I remember all kinds of wailing and kitchy-kitchy-cooing. After fifteen minutes of this I had to sit down, so my friends got me a chair and some food and came over to talk to me. The irony was not lost on any of us of a baby on her first steps in life and a man possibly on the first steps in death. Half the people in the room were doctors. Before the last guest was gone, I went upstairs to bed and slept the entire afternoon.

They removed the catheter three days later at the hospital and I celebrated with the Best Pee in My Life. As with most cancer surgeries, the stage following involves chemotherapy. But with bladder cancer, the chemo isn't some poisonous brew cooked up by scientists. It's tuberculosis. You read that right. It's called BCG (Bacillus Calmette-Guérin), which causes TB, though, as cancer.org points out, "... it doesn't usually cause serious disease."

It's injected up your penis once a week over six weeks. You can't pee for two hours after and when you do, you need to immediately pour bleach into the toilet and let it sit for fifteen minutes before flushing. The second you pee, though, you need to scrub your hands thoroughly and put bleach on anything, like the toilet rim, that your pee may have dribbled onto.

This was hell on many levels.

The first time Dr. Radomski injected the BCG up my penis, I started to sweat and feel faint. I had to stay laid down on the gurney for half an hour, and when I got up I was still wobbly. No one said this would happen. Would I have to take an entire day off once a week for six weeks to deal with the side effects? That turned out not to be the case as I built up a tolerance for the stuff each time I went. I'd forgotten that "chemo" for millions of other people is a good deal more stressful and sickening than this.

The instructions for peeing and bleaching were stern and complex. So that first time, I had my giant bottle of bleach at the ready at home for my first pee. Ouch! That stings. Now, pour the bleach quickly into the ...

My phone rang. It was Jean.

"Hi dear, what's up?"

"I just want to check in on how you're doing."

"Well, I just peed and poured the bleach into the toilet and ... uh ..." I was doing up my pants as I spoke to her "... I'm checking for any drops of pee to make sure I don't have TB."

"Honey," Jean said slowly. "You do have TB. They *injected* you with TB. The bleach is not about you. It's about me and the people of Toronto to make sure we don't get TB when you flush it down the toilet into the water system."

"Oh."

It didn't take long for me to get used to this whole process. After each injection, I'd head to work, wait two hours to pee, take my tiny bottle of bleach, pour it in, sit on the toilet with my laptop, and work for fifteen minutes.

The actual injection was no fun, of course, but Dr. Radomski and his nurses were easy and friendly. One time, though, Radomski wasn't there, replaced by a younger resident who was clearly trying hard to impress the nurses. Just as he was about to insert the catheter into me, he stopped and asked, "Have you filled out your consent form?" Yes, I had. I always did that in advance. They insisted on it.

"Did you read it?"

"Uh, no, I didn't."

"You should, you know."

Of course I knew. But I'm lying down on a gurney with a catheter about to be jammed up my penis and I'm going to discuss the ramifications of a document I'd signed half a dozen times? Who was this guy kidding?

Then, after he'd pulled the catheter out and I was putting on my underwear, he said, "One piece of advice, Mr. Ramsay. You may not be wanting to have sex today, if you know what I mean."

Good advice, doctor. Because at this very moment what I want to do most in my life is have a roll in the hay. I'm totally up for that.

After six weeks of injections, I had a cystoscopy. This is to your penis what a colonoscopy is to your bowel. They inject a tube up your penis with a tiny camera (and lights!) attached. Then the doctor explores your bladder the way a submersible does the ocean floor, in search of tumours or inflammation in your bladder wall. Inflammation is the precursor to all kinds of cancers. Dr. Radomski saw some, as did I because the patient can see this whole exploration on the screen, too.

"You see here? … It's redder than the rest … Now, that could be caused by the BCG because it kind of scorches everything … or it could be something we should worry about. I think we should continue with the BCG for six more weeks."

This six weeks of injections followed by a cystoscopy continued for the first half of 2015. The inflammation didn't grow. But it didn't go away, either. So Dr. Radomski ordered up a biopsy where they snip a bit of your bladder and send it off to the lab to see if it's cancerous. It wasn't. Every so often he'd put me back on six weeks of BCG injections just to keep things tamped down in case that redness was cancerous.

As well, during the cystoscopies he'd do something called a cyto-wash, which can indicate if a tumour is growing.

In the four years since I started having cystoscopies, I've moved from one every three months to one every six. This is good. I've also had more biopsies and cyto-washes because while the inflammation isn't spreading, it isn't going away, either.

When I met with Dr. Radomski in March of 2018 for my latest cystoscopy, he said, "Come in to my office after; we can discuss your biopsy results."

Uh-oh. He never discussed the previous two, though this latest was a double biopsy with two snips. He was always so "up" that I couldn't read if this was the "I have bad news" conversation. We sat down in his tiny office and he said, "Your biopsy's negative."

Whew.

"It's a bit of a mystery why the inflammation just sits there. But look, you've had three biopsies and four cyto-washes, and they're all negative. So either you're clear ... or you're the unluckiest guy in the world."

21 Girls with Sharp Knives

One rule of joining a new family is to embrace their traditions with gusto.

In 1990, Jean invited me to come to her annual Christmas party. Or rather her Italian Catholic–Christmas Eve–Fish Dinner.

She's neither Italian nor Catholic and the party was held a week before Christmas. Oh well, apparently this was all part of learning a new family language.

The next year, after I'd moved in with Jean and the kids, I got to help organize the party. The day before, Jean said, "Can you come with me to pick up the eels?"

"What?"

"The eels. They're part of the meal. You can barbeque them."

Again, I was baffled at these odd family customs.

We drove to the Portuguese fish market in Toronto's west end, where a young man greeted Jean like an old friend and said, "Half a dozen?" He then dipped a long pole with a big net into a large vat of water, catching a slither of live eels in the net. He grabbed one with his glove and put it into a white plastic bag filled with water. Then another and another. We left with two bags, three eels in each bag. Jean put them in the back of the car with the shrimp and salmon.

There was one difference, though. Those fish were dead. The eels were alive. This vaguely bothered me as I wondered who would end their lives and how. Halfway home, Jean called her daughters to say she had to stop by the hospital to pick something up before we got home. Yes, she had the eels, she said. We drove to the front of Women's College hospital, where Jean said, "Back in a sec." Five minutes later, she was back and we headed home.

"What did you pick up?"

"Scalpels."

"What for?"

"The eels."

My heart raced.

"You're ... going ... to ...?"

"It's a Christmas tradition. Lara, MaryBeth, and I behead them, then prep them for the barbeque."

"What about Jean Paul?"

"He stays away. This is a girls' thing."

Staying away struck me as the smartest thing Jean Paul had ever done. I could learn from him.

"A girls' thing?"

"Do you want to help?"

"No!"

"I want you to barbeque them tomorrow, though."

I did have to take the two bags of eels downstairs when we got home. The girls took the bags and expertly dumped the eels into the laundry tub where they splashed about, oblivious to their fate.

Then Charlie the golden retriever came to the basement at the exact moment one of the eels leapt over the edge of the tub and landed on the floor. Charlie pounced, barely missing his prey.

I ran upstairs and almost ran into Jean Paul.

"What's going on downstairs?"

"Charlie's after one of the eels."

"Right. Today's eel day."

"I guess."

He then turned on his heel and went upstairs. I heard muffled noises from Jean and her daughters in the basement ... and decided I, too, would go upstairs. Denial can be a real lifesaver.

22 "I Want to Be a Preacher"

Brent Hawkes gives me a big hug at our Christmas party. He's one of seventy-five guests crammed into our Toronto condo. It's 2016, and for the past year he's been dealing with sexual assault charges that might put him in jail for the rest of his life. The judge's decision will come down in January.

Brent leans in to say, "Bob, I've had all kinds of counsel on how to handle this. But no matter what the verdict is, I just want to say that your advice to xvxnnemq yemmmm emmmmmm was by far the most ennnti ammme dywisne."

"What?"

What's he saying!? I lean closer to catch what I've missed when, with his eyes now tearing up, he plants a big kiss on my cheek. "Thank you. Thank you!"

Christ! I couldn't hear those last critical words and my memory is so shot that it's futile trying to remember what advice I gave him over a year ago. Worse, this was such a satisfying emotional moment for Brent (and was meant to be for me) that I felt embarrassed to ask him to repeat himself. So I didn't. I just smiled and hugged him back and muttered something like "You're the one we should be thanking." He glowed.

I first saw Brent in action twenty-five years ago, when Jean and I were headed to a Christmas Eve skating party with some friends who lived downtown near city hall.

We knocked on their door at 9:00 p.m., as instructed. No answer. Odd. Knocked again. Nothing. Peered into the windows. Dark. Right address? Yup. Been there many times before. Right Christmas Eve? Hard to get that wrong. In any case, we were out in the cold with nothing to do except drive home. That drive took us past Roy Thomson Hall, which was all lit up with lots of people inside. The sign said, "Metropolitan Community Church Carol Service, 9:30 p.m. Free."

Well, hey, we'd always loved carols, and back in high school I was the head choirboy, and those harmonies have held sway this time every year since. So in we went.

We were way early, but the lobbies were packed. I found it odd that lots of women came up to Jean and thanked her for coming. They were surprised and happy that their doctor was showing her support, and said so. Support for what? I wondered.

My confusion was cleared up once we joined the 2,500 others who streamed inside for the carol service. Onstage were a small orchestra and a choir. In the wings stood a gnomish man with bright red robes and a devilish smile. He strode to the podium to welcome us all to the MCC Christmas carol service.

This was a church service? Yes. Did he mean Metropolitan United Church? No. It became clear that MCC was Toronto's gay church, that the man at the podium was Brent Hawkes, and that the women who came up to Jean beforehand viewed her being there as an act of overt political support from their doctor. Remember, this was twenty-five years ago, when showing your colours was not so easy.

The choir was glorious and we all bellowed our hearts out. But I was mesmerized by how Brent spoke: he was funny, angry, and determined. He asked the parents of those in the audience to stand up while we applauded them for being there. Parents didn't stand up easily or quickly, then. You could tell a lot of them were from small towns, who'd come to see their kids in the big city for Christmas. Many looked distinctly uncomfortable standing there, as if exposing yourself as the parent of a gay child was an act worthy of deep shame. Until ... well, until the entire place started clapping and cheering for them. Most parents now smiled. A few wept. Some were even more confused.

I was hooked. On Brent Hawkes, on the music, on the whole experience. Forget figure skating. We simply had to come back here next Christmas Eve — and bring our friends.

It was midnight before the service ended, and getting from our seats to the street outside was like watching a Pride Parade with winter clothing on. How did I see those incredible outfits now and miss them when I walked in?

We walked to our car, which I'd parked four storeys below ground in a building across the street. By now, we were truly infected with the Christmas spirit and the God of Chance who let us stumble on this treasure. So, rather than take the elevator, we decided to walk down the four floors to our car. At the third level down,

I heard footsteps behind me. Uh-oh. They grew closer. I glanced back. There were two very big men, dressed in S&M leathers and chains, almost on us. I told Jean to hurry up and pulled out my car keys in case I had to poke their eyes out.

By the time we reached the fourth floor, they were just yards away. I wheeled around and said loudly, "Can I help you?!"

To which one replied, "Merry Christmas. Wasn't that a great service?!"

So it was that I invited Brent Hawkes to speak at a RamsayTalks luncheon a few months later. One of my pet hates is fast-talking evangelists using the pulpit of the Church of What's Happening Now to fleece their parishioners in the name of the Lord.

Brent was not that and neither was MCC. He'd earned his Doctor of Divinity from the most established institution in Canada, Trinity College at the University of Toronto. This also meant he was an Anglican at heart, as was I.

In 2001 he also performed the first legal same-sex marriage in the world from the altar of MCC, which is in the heart of Toronto's Riverdale neighbourhood. And, as I learned over the years, if ever there was a poor church mouse of a community-service organization, it's MCC.

Meanwhile, when I looked at the list of attendees at the RamsayTalks luncheon where Brent was to speak, most of them were older and very established businessmen, like Harry Rosen. My sense was they had signed up to hear an argument from a man rising in the news — and to leave disagreeing with him. But Brent didn't talk about the gay movement in terms of sexuality at all. For him, it was strictly about human rights. If you're against the gay rights movement, you're against what makes you human.

And how can any religious organization — especially those who say, "hate the sin, love the sinner" — work to keep gays out? It's exactly like casting out people who are not your colour.

I'm sure in the movement this is a time-worn argument. But Brent's refusal to even consider the gay rights issue as anything other than a human rights issue made a powerful impression on me and those stone-faced businessmen.

Every year since then, Jean and I have taken groups of friends to the MCC Carol Service. Sometimes I would invite people who I knew would rather do anything than spend their Christmas Eve with thousands of gays. I never hinted at that, however. I just said it was the "MCC Carol Service at Roy Thomson Hall." One year, we had our twenty-four guests back to our home after the service for a light supper. This meant it was 1:00 a.m. Christmas Day before we dug in. Harry Rosen was there, and when he took me aside to ask, "Bob, who are all these people?" I replied, "Orphans and Jews, Harry. Orphans and Jews."

He laughed because he was headed south later Christmas Day to join his wife in Florida. But MCC was growing on Harry, and he soon made a sizable personal donation to the church. I thought of calling our annual Christmas Eve party Orphans and Jews, but saner heads prevailed.

One day years later I got a call at the office from Brent. He asked if I had a few minutes to chat. Sure. He said that the congregation wanted to hear more about their own concerns from the pulpit, and had proposed that once a month for the next year an outsider be invited to speak on their area of expertise. "So, Bob, I'm wondering if you'd like to give a sermon."

"Me? ... Uh ..."

I didn't have a clue why he was asking. I'd given talks on giving presentations, on running marathons, and once (dreadfully) on networking.

"Brent, whatever do you want me to speak about?"

"Addiction."

He quickly filled the ensuing silence. "You've never talked to me about it, Bob, but I hear from lots of people you have talked to. So if you're willing ..."

I panicked.

It was one thing to talk to 12-Step groups about addiction. I've sat in literally hundreds of meetings in church basements, hospitals, and community halls all over Toronto, Atlanta, and Penetang, and felt totally at home in them.

In fact, that's what Step 12 is: "To carry this message to alcoholics and addicts like me." And, of course, lots of those same friends who knew Brent knew that for two years in 1989–90 I was not only dependent on cocaine; it ruled me. But those talks were always one to one, over coffee with fellow addicts, not "out" in front of hundreds of strangers.

This was.

"Bob, you'd give the same sermon at our two services on Sunday morning, one at 9:00 a.m. and the other at 11:00 a.m. The later one usually gets five hundred people. You need to know the gay community has a closer relationship to drugs and alcohol than most. Shame is still a huge issue, of course, as is the rave party scene with drugs like 'poppers' used for recreational sex. But staying in the closet sexually has lots of parallels about staying in the closet around drug and alcohol abuse."

"Uh ... Brent, give me a day to think about this, okay, and I'll get back to you tomorrow." I was going to chicken out.

On my way home that night, I remembered that Brent had said not to talk so much about my own addiction, but what it could teach the congregation. What advice did I have for someone who thinks a family member or colleague is in trouble? What if they end up in jail? In hospital? Dead?

When I got home, I mentioned Brent's phone call to Jean and said I didn't think I should do it.

"Of course you should. You must!"

Her reaction caught me by surprise.

"Why?"

"You owe it to your friends and family. I'll make sure we'll all be there."

Right. I'd forgotten the step that talked about gratitude. The fact is, I hadn't recovered on my own. Jean and dozens of friends had helped me, especially in the first six months after I got home from treatment in Atlanta.

Sure, I'd often entertained friends over coffee with tales of advancing from my treatment to being a therapist-intern at a centre for crack addicts in inner-city Atlanta.

But I'd never stood up in front of five hundred people and said, "My name's Bob and I'm an addict." Nor did I think I should tell a group of people I wasn't part of how addiction affects them specifically.

"Okay, I'll do it."

And so it was that on a Sunday morning in the fall of 2010, I walked to the pulpit of the Metropolitan Community Church and said to the three hundred or so people gathered for the 9:00 a.m. service ...

Thank you, Brent, for asking me to speak this morning on the tantalizing and demonized subject of addiction.

Twenty years ago, when I was freshly clean and sober, I was invited by a friend to a gala hosted by the then Clarke Institute of Psychiatry. It was their second annual "Courage to Come Back Dinner," celebrating people who have come back from mental illness. They decided to add a new category that year, which was addictions.

When the winner was announced, the man seated on my left turned to me and muttered,

"Jesus Christ, now they're giving out prizes for being a goddamn drug addict!"

I wondered how the word *goddamn* would go over from the
pulpit. But everyone laughed, even Brent. I was used to talking to
large groups and enjoyed giving my introductions to the speakers at
RamsayTalks. But this was different, somehow.

First of all, I was perched very high up, looking down on everyone.
I didn't need to look up to the balcony because no one was there. Also,
writing the sermon in the days before had been incredibly easy. The
only research I did was to find when the American Medical Association
declared that alcoholism was a disease and not a character flaw (1957)
and when their Canadian counterparts came to the same conclusion
(1963). For the rest of my half-hour talk on what to do when heavy
alcohol and drug use enters your world, the words flowed fluently and
far. After all, I was the authority, and I spoke from on high.

Disturbing numbers of people still believe — deep
down where their words are spoken only to themselves — that addiction, like homosexuality, is not
a state of being, but a badge of shame. And because
what we believe is different from what we say, it's
no surprise that addiction is one of the last great
afflictions to be dragged out of the closet.

After all, when one of our friends can't stop
putting chemicals into their body, we wonder
one thing: Why are they so weak? Where is their
willpower? I mean, they're about to lose their job,
their mate, their house — no, now they're in jail,
in the psych ward, in the morgue.

I was headed there myself. In 1990, after two
years of persistent cocaine use, I had lost my

business, my house, certainly my self-respect. I
would do incredibly dangerous things. I would
swear after each all-night binge that I would never
use drugs again. And I would fail.

I couldn't understand it — I have huge willpower, so why could I not stop? I was desperate
to. But I was also desperate to use, and my shame
at not being able to control my actions drove me
into even greater use, which made me more desperate, which ... well, that's the cycle of addiction
unchecked.

I've never met a happy cocaine addict. Every
addict is, by definition, unhappy, running away
from a thousand different kinds of pain, and using
drugs or booze to make the pain disappear, which
only makes it worse.

At age forty, I was smiling on the outside, but
crying on the inside, not knowing what a feeling
even was, yet terrified they would sweep me away.

I only stopped because some friends intervened
on me, and frogmarched me to a treatment centre
in the U.S. If those friends hadn't been there, I
wouldn't be here.

By the time I was done, I was on a roll. I'd written my conclusion for maximum effect, ending on the idea that, just as addiction
is a family disease, recovery is all about the very thing that MCC is
about — community.

When someone is so far gone that they can't act
for themselves, someone has to step in and take
action. If that someone is you, have faith — you

can do it, the same way the addict you're trying to help can. By reaching out for help. By
talking and by reconnecting. Because the family
and friends of addicts are also alone. And what is
community but never having to be alone?

Finished, I looked up.
Silence.
Uh-oh.
Then applause. Loud applause. Whistles. Feet stomping.
In a church.
You know what I felt that very second?
High.
I sat back down in the front pew from where I stood up half an
hour earlier and knew something had changed.

During the reception after the service, all kinds of people came
up to thank me for helping them. Their brother had OD'd on
heroin. Their best friend was living on the street. As for themselves ... well, here's an odd thing. I learned from giving my same
sermon to business groups in the years afterward that two kinds
of people gather round you in concentric circles after any talk on
alcoholism and addiction. There's the inner circle, the people who
come right up to you, maybe even introduce themselves and tell
you their story — but it's always about someone else. The people
in the second circle a few feet back, they're the ones I really want
to talk to. They're the ones with the problem. But there's no way
they're going to be caught talking directly to someone like me
because others may see us and say, "Hmmm ... I wonder if Mary
has a problem."

Then it was back into the church for the 11:00 a.m. service. This
was the one Jean said she'd be at. She wasn't the only one. There must
have been five hundred people there, some hanging from the rafters. I

knew they hadn't come to hear me. They'd just slept in and came to the later service. Jean and I sat in the front row and Brent introduced me.

But this time when I said, "Thank you, Brent, for asking me to speak ..." I knew it would be different. I was totally at ease. I knew what to pump up, what to tone down. I knew when to pause, not to get the laugh, but to draw it out. I paused between paragraphs, not fearing my silence, but working it.

The only thing that slowed me down was Jean. She was sitting dead centre in front and below me. The first time I looked at her, she was crying. For a second I thought, *Oh my god, what have I done to her? This is such a mistake.* But she soon smiled through her tears and kept smiling for the entire sermon.

Then, for the second time that morning, I came to the end of my sermon.

Again, silence, followed by whistling and stomping — and this time, cheering.

Wait, what are they doing? They're standing up and clapping!

I did this? I couldn't believe it. But it seems, yes, I got a standing ovation, in a church, for a sermon.

I looked down at my hands. They were shaking. Uh-oh. The last time that happened was when I was so stoned on cocaine I couldn't hold a glass to drink out of it. I smiled and quickly stepped down from the podium, my arms tightly by my sides. It was on that ten-yard walk back to the centre pew that my legs started to shake, as well.

So I dived into my seat beside Jean, grabbing her hands with mine and holding on tight. By this time, she was blubbery with tears. We held each other as everyone sat back down around us. She asked, "Are you all right, dear?"

"I'm fine, darling ..." Then I leaned close to her ear and whispered, "I want to be a preacher!"

I remember walking home with Jean after the service and the reception where we were both greeted like conquering heroes. On our walk up to Danforth on that beautiful October Sunday, I couldn't stop talking about how it felt to be in the pulpit.

A few blocks from our home I noticed a couple of young men following us. Not randomly. They seemed to be talking about us. As we went into the Starbucks on Danforth, they came in a few seconds later, both still looking at us. I turned to them and said, "Hey, what's up with you guys?"

"We heard you in church and just wanted to thank you. You and your wife walk pretty fast, but we want to shake your hands because I think you just saved my life."

"Oh ... uh ... thank you."

Such it was that Brent Hawkes married our son Jean Paul and daughter-in-law Kate ten years later and baptized their daughter three years ago and their son ... well, that baptism was planned for a couple of weeks after our Christmas Party. But Brent's verdict wasn't in. In fact, though, that was firmly sorted out. Right after Brent praised my advice on how to handle his trial — that time when I could neither quite make out what he was saying nor remember what advice I might have given — Jean Paul came up to Brent with Wyatt Grayson Marmoreo in his arms to tell his baby son that this bearded man was going to pour some water on him in a church.

And, a month later, a judge in New Brunswick declared the Rev. Brent Hawkes innocent of the sexual assault charges, citing "significant inconsistencies in the testimony of the witnesses."

23 Four Men and a Wedding

You know the game where you put together a dinner party with the most fascinating people in your circle? Your country? Human history? All the guests have to be compelling in their own right and have to create sparks with the others at the table. Nancy Pelosi and Donald Trump. Margaret Atwood and Doug Ford. Oscar Wilde and Boris Johnson. Meghan Markle and Kate Middleton.

That kind of dinner actually happened to me. It wasn't a game, but the wedding dinner of my stepson Jean Paul Marmoreo and his wife, Kate Hood, in 2012. At our table were three very close men friends: Dan O'Connor, a retired U.S. Marine major; the Rev. Brent Hawkes, who had performed the first same-sex marriage in the world as well as today's wedding; and Costa Pilavachi, a recording impresario whose clients included the leading lights of the classical music world, from Pavarotti to Hvorostovsky.

These men had wildly different sets of values and experience. I was the glue among them. Costa was my roommate in the seventies, Dan was the champion of JeansMarines, and Brent persuaded me to talk about addiction in a sermon to his parishioners. They all knew Jean very well and adored her; and they'd got to know Jean Paul through us. We considered them part of our extended family.

Here's what brought them to the table.

In 1974, I was working as a speech writer in the office of Ontario premier William Davis. I was going out with Liz Dunlop, the daughter-in-law of a colleague of mine.

Liz was nice and normal. She had a female friend named Eleni who was anything but: a gorgeous Greek woman who gave new definition to the idea of high-strung. Back then, a big part of our social lives was going for late-night coffee at the Courtyard Café, then one of the hot dining places in Toronto, in the Windsor Arms Hotel. We couldn't possibly afford to have dinner there, but the maître d' would let us in for late-night coffee if it wasn't crowded.

One night Liz's friend was gushing on — and on — about her cousin, a Greek guy who had just moved to Toronto. His father had been the Greek ambassador to Canada and he was brought up in the Château Laurier Hotel, which was the ambassador's residence. He'd taken the arts administration course at York and had just started working at Haber Artists Management, Canada's first agency for classical artists, from Karen Kain to Famous People Players. Liz's friend insisted I meet him because I would absolutely *love* him. "You're so *alike*." Who was she kidding?

"Sounds like a piece of Eurotrash to me." I hated him already.

Meanwhile, she was saying exactly the same things to Costa Pilavachi about me.

"Smart, into everything, Princeton, Premier's Office, etc." He had the same reaction. "Sounds like an insufferable WASP to me." But she was persistent, and one night Costa and I turned up at the Courtyard Café to be introduced by our matchmaker.

We were wary. Our blood was up. But within five minutes, it came down. Costa was incredibly charming, funny, and smart. He also seemed that rarest of all things, nice.

By the time our second coffees arrived, we'd ceased even trying to keep Eleni in the conversation and talked only to and about each other. From that night on, Costa and I were fast friends.

Six months later, Costa mentioned in passing that we should consider moving into a house together. It would be him and me and we should find a couple of others so we could save on rent. "Who do you have in mind?" I asked. "How about Helga Stephenson. She's started working in our office and she's looking, too. She just got back from a year teaching at the University of Havana."

She sounded a little exotic.

"I'll have her call you." Helga did call the next day and, in our five-minute conversation, she managed to scare the hell out of me. Who was this supremely confident woman? And what exactly did she teach at the University of Havana? With her and Costa, I was entering a world beyond my pay grade.

She also had a name to complete our foursome in the house that ... well, nobody'd actually got around to finding yet. But something would turn up for me and Costa and Helga and the fourth member of our strange band, who proved to be Debbie Kirshner, a violinist.

It only took a week to find an old red-brick home in Cabbagetown, just east off Parliament Street. The rent was $145 each per month, and we all brought our own furniture.

It's the kind of place you want to live in only in your twenties, and we did for three years. Slightly rundown, more like a college dorm, four bedrooms and one bathroom, and great for parties.

Helga was very close to the famed Cuban dancer Alicia Alonso, who headed the National Ballet of Cuba. She encouraged them to dance in Toronto and Montreal, a tour made all the easier because Helga spoke fluent Spanish and French. She was also a distant cousin of the Eaton family, as she would say, "on the poor Icelandic side." She would often fly down to Cuba to make arrangements for the tour here, and one night the phone rang and it was Helga calling from Havana. It was hard to hear her. But the gist was that I should call her cousin Fred Eaton and tell him to have fifty air conditioners at the back door of what was then the O'Keefe Centre after the Cubans' final performance in two weeks.

It seemed that giving each dancer an air conditioner to take home was part of the deal Helga had negotiated with Alicia Alonso. And, I was told, don't ask Fred Eaton. Tell him.

So the next day I gathered up my best stammer and called the CEO of Eaton's and passed on Helga's request. He asked for her number in Cuba, thanked me, and hung up.

And so it was that at eleven o'clock one winter's night, an Eaton's truck turned up outside the stage door to the O'Keefe Centre and offloaded fifty top-of-the-line air conditioners from Eaton's.

It seemed Helga had all sorts of side deals with the Cubans. One summer night, I walked home late from my job in the Premier's Office. It was around ten o'clock and I could see ahead a number of black cars parked on both sides of the curb outside our house. What was this?

As I got closer, I saw that the cars on the house side all had license plates with the letters *CDA*, which is the universal signifier for members of the diplomatic corps. Not *CCA*, which is the consular corps, of which there were many dozens driving around

Toronto. *CDA* meant they'd all driven down from Ottawa. Who could they be?

I got closer. The two cars on the south side of the street both had their engines running and there were men inside them. They were all looking at our house. Odd.

I walked into my house and there were twenty people dancing to Cuban music, which was very loud. It was hot and many of the partiers looked drunk. It was a Monday, which inflamed my rising sense of insult. *Christ, I'll never get any sleep.* So I went upstairs to my bedroom, opened the door and … there was a man and a woman in my bed, having sex.

Helga!

She'd invited the Cubans down to Toronto for an afternoon of cultural negotiations and an evening party at her place. She called some women friends and offered them a Cuban party with real Cubans. The guys across the street were from the RCMP, tailing the Cuban diplomats, some of whom *were* spies, from Ottawa.

It offended me and thrilled me at the same time. So this was how the world worked.

Clearly, it was; because Helga went on to help build the Toronto International Film Festival to one of the biggest and best in the world. Her deal-making and party-hosting skills were honed early on with us.

In fact, Costa dubbed our place "the fornicatorium," and on many mornings we played a game where we had to guess who the new man or woman was in the bathroom without asking anybody who they'd been with the night before.

While none of us was lacking in social skills, we weren't much good at homemaking skills. One winter's Saturday night, Costa and I were at home watching the Toronto Maple Leafs hockey game on TV. It seemed a bit chilly in the house, so we each put on sweaters. The game was exciting, in part because of the novelty of being home on a Saturday night and watching TV — something we never did. So this was *Hockey Night in Canada*! By the third period, the house was really cold and we could see our breath. We both put on our winter parkas as we drank beer and ate popcorn, our eyes glued to the TV.

Suddenly, the front door opened and in walked Helga carrying her suitcase from a tour somewhere. We looked up and said, "Hi, want to watch the game?"

"The game! Are you guys crazy? It's freezing in here! For Christ's sake, I can see my breath! What have you done?!"

Costa and I gazed across at each other, as if to say, "What's wrong with her?," then went back to watching the game.

A few minutes later, Helga came up from the basement and announced, "You fucking idiots. We're out of heating oil. You let the tank run down to zero."

Again, we looked at each other, then back to the game.

"We'll call them tomorrow," Costa said. "It's not that cold. Come on and watch the game with us."

"Tomorrow is Sunday. Call. Them. Now!"

"Okay, okay."

One night many years after our joint household had blown apart from its own manic energy, Costa was living in Amsterdam, where he headed the Philips Classics record label. It was 1998, and Jean and I had gathered a group of friends for a big trip together. We would go on to do more of these, but on this first one, eight of us would try to summit Mount Kilimanjaro in Tanzania and then all do a safari together. Our way station was Amsterdam, where we'd recover from jet lag and see the sights. Costa hosted us all at dinner at his home one night. Three walls of his living room were stacked floor to ceiling with CDs. He was in the business, after all. As the wine flowed, so did our patriotism. Jean asked how the Toronto Symphony stacked up against the Berlin Philharmonic?

"They're a fourth-rate band."

Ouch.

Costa was always charming but could be tough about business and implacable about quality, two values it would take me years to even start to learn.

"What do you mean?!" Jean didn't know much about classical music, but she knew what she liked. She also wanted proof and wasn't about to let Costa dismiss her just because she was an outsider.

"I mean," said Costa, "you can tell the difference just by comparing how they play thirty seconds of something."

"Like what?"

"Well, you tell me. Pick a piece."

"Handel's *Messiah*." Their swords were drawn. We all stopped talking as Costa left the table, went over to his wall of CDs, and picked out four versions of the *Messiah*. One was with the Boston Symphony, where he'd served as artistic administrator for many years; one with the Berlin Philharmonic; one with the Montreal Symphony Orchestra; and the final one, with the Toronto Symphony Orchestra.

He then took all four CDs out of their covers and painstakingly found the same musical phrase in each performance on the CD timer and wrote the time down.

He was putting together a show.

"Ready? Okay, everyone listen hard to each one."

We did, and you know what, we could actually hear the difference between Berlin and Toronto. We all had to agree that Berlin was better, as was Boston and even Montreal. Toronto wasn't awful, but, by this test, it *was* a fourth-rate band.

We also learned a lesson in listening, and what it takes to work at the top of your profession — or to have the skills to enjoy the difference in their sounds, and to care so very much.

Believe me, a foodie, a tennis fan, or a oenophile would be no less adamant when it came to judging excellence.

While we were sheepish because we were all from Toronto, Costa had opened a door for all of us. So the next day when Costa led us on a bike ride and picnic on the Amstel River, I asked Costa who the rising stars in the classical world were. This was like asking a successful broker, "What are the stocks you're interested in?"

Without skipping a beat, Costa said, "Oh, Valery Gergiev for sure. If he's not the best, he's the most exciting."

None of us had ever heard this name. Gergiev conducted the Kirov Orchestra in St. Petersburg. In fact, he was the general director of the Kirov Opera and the Kirov Ballet, as well. The Philips label had signed Gergiev and his orchestra back in 1991, the same year the Soviet Union collapsed. "Mark my word," Costa said, "in ten years, he'll be the most famous conductor in the world. In fact, he's just started a summer festival in St. Petersburg called the White Nights. We should all go."

Now how many times have we been together with friends, maybe over more wine than cheese, and one of them says, "Next year, we should all …" do something exotic or far away.

We all nod our heads and say, "Great idea." And nothing ever happens, because life always intervenes. But not with Costa and, more and more, not with me. I'd known Jean for eight years now and been married to her for five, and everything about my life was better than before I met her on that strange encounter at Carolyn Bennett's cottage when the adults' boat ride took longer than it should have, and Jean and I were forced to make burgers together.

I was still going to AA meetings, though not the ninety meetings in ninety days I'd been ordered to when I was released from Talbott in September of 1990. My life as an addict felt so long ago and far away. I know — that's when thoughts of relapsing enter your head.

But they honestly never did for me. I'd crave a cold beer when I would run by a bar in the summer training for a fall marathon. But cocaine, no.

It was also clear from our summer on the Appalachian Trail, and our annual "destination" marathons, that we both loved adventure on the road. The more Jean and I travelled, the more we loved to travel, especially to exotic places, and we were in great shape, too. Jean's kids were finally all grown up and gone from the nest, as well. So now, by 1999, we had the three things that are crucial if you're going to think of making travel a big part of your life: time (kids gone!), health, and money. Jean made a good living as a doctor, of course, and I'd joined a communications consulting firm when I got back from treatment. Four years later, chafing at not being able to write as much as I'd liked, I left and went out on my own. Thus was born Ramsay Writes, whose name I changed a few years later to Ramsay Inc. because I was now doing writing and much more. I was hosting writers in something I'd christened RamsayTalks. These names weren't part of some grand corporate strategy. I didn't set out to turn what had been a hobby into a business. But RamsayTalks today *is* a business.

But as I often say these days, I'm a writer with a lot of lipstick. And it's the corporate writing that's given me the standard of living to improve my standard of life.

But five of us finding ourselves the next year at a music festival in Russia? That wasn't my doing. It was Costa's. He cajoled us to go, explaining it was called the White Nights because, in June, the sun only sets for three hours in St. Petersburg. Besides, he would say over and over, you've never heard musicians or dancers or singers this good.

The first clue came on our first night at the festival, which was held in the old Mariinsky Theatre, opened in 1860, some seventy-seven years after Catherine the Great had decreed a theatre to "direct plays and music." As we walked into this gorgeous nineteenth century opera house, the ushers, who could spot that we weren't Russian from far away, handed us a folded sheet with purple ink that had been Gestetnered for our use. Ah, I remember the smell of that ink from elementary school in Edmonton! It was the concert program, written in broken English. And on the front cover, it said: "Welcome to our 216th season."

Hmmmm ... It seems they've been doing this a lot longer than we have. Maybe they're ... Well, the Kirov Orchestra (now called the Mariinsky) that night wasn't just great. It was stupendous. We'd never heard a sound so big and clean and commanding. We were thrown back in our seats. As for Valery Gergiev ... he was mesmerizing. When the concert was done, Jean and I and our three friends rose for the inevitable standing ovation, only to discover we were the only ones standing. Even Costa beside us sat through the applause. Tough crowd.

When everyone was streaming out of the theatre, Costa said, "Let's go backstage to meet Valery. Then we should take him to dinner."

Backstage, maybe. But dinner?

We dined with Gergiev on two of the four nights we were there.

Why? Because otherwise he'd be eating alone. We were friends of Costa, the record label chief who was upping Gergiev's exposure in the lucrative West. The only other person with us was Gergiev's bodyguard, who was his brother.

Unlike many artists, Gergiev is endlessly curious about other people. The almost demonic focus in his eyes simply reflects what's on his mind. He talked for what seemed like hours with Jean, the woman doctor who ran marathons. Maybe it *was* hours, because these dinners went on until the sun started to set around two in the morning. They would be the first of many such late-night bacchanals. We quickly learned that when a professional artist has performed onstage, they're not exhausted afterward. They're high.

We left St. Petersburg with a new appreciation for quality — in classical music, in opera, in ballet. We were by no means experts in appreciating these art forms. But even we could tell what a huge difference a tint difference makes at the highest levels of performance.

Costa had introduced us to a world that would turn out to be rich in sounds, in people, and in adventures.

Two years later, Costa called me to say that Gergiev was bringing the Mariinsky Orchestra to its first tour of America and he wanted one of the stops to be in Toronto. The problem was, every performance needed a local sponsor. Touring orchestras is never cheap. Sadly, 2001 was the year the Toronto Symphony Orchestra nearly went bankrupt. So no bank or other company was going to sponsor an unknown orchestra with an unknown conductor in a concert of unfamiliar Russian music.

But Jean and I and our three friends knew what no one else did. We knew how incredibly good the Mariinsky was. If we could just help get them here ...

"What does the sponsorship cost?"

"Twenty-five thousand dollars."

I went home that night and put the idea to Jean. If we all each chipped in five thousand dollars, the Mariinsky could premiere at Roy Thomson Hall in Toronto.

While that wasn't a lot of money for our three friends, it was for us. It's also a tiny fraction of what sponsoring the Mariinsky costs today. But looking back on the twenty-year friendship we've had with Valery Gergiev — and the astonishing things that grew from it — that sponsorship was the best investment of our lives.

The Mariinsky's concert in Roy Thomson Hall sold out days ahead. The performance was unforgettable. I personally sold two hundred of the 2,500 tickets, a lot of them to friends who dragged along spouses who would far rather be at a Leafs game. One of them buttonholed me as the crowds were pouring out of Roy Thomson afterward and said, "I don't know what I just heard, but it was incredible!"

We never forgot it. More important, Gergiev never forgot that the nice Canadians he'd had dinner with two years earlier in St. Petersburg made it happen for him. Gergiev isn't just a loyal guy, he's tribal in his loyalty. Maybe it's because he's not actually Russian; he's Ossetian, from the tiny republic next to another FSR (Former Soviet Republic), Chechnya.

So Jean and I over the years have found ourselves at opening nights, glittering balls, and strange Moscow restaurants wondering what we're doing there at two in the morning. We are definitely not his crowd. Maybe that's why we keep getting invited. We're not power players or oligarchs. We're also not favour-seekers, which anyone at his level becomes surrounded with.

He doesn't have the smallest ego on earth. But at least it's open-ended and invites you in. One day I was walking near Lincoln Center in New York and there, having lunch on a patio, was Gergiev. He greeted me like a long-lost friend and asked me if I was free. I should meet him in half an hour in the lobby of his apartment. He had something to show me.

So up we went together where he showed me his new toy. It was the portfolio of drawings done by a Los Angeles architect for a new development he was fronting in St. Petersburg. It would be on an island on the Neva River that cut through the city. On this island Gergiev wanted to have a Four Seasons Hotel, luxury shopping, apartments, and, most of all, a new Mariinsky Theatre. The one we'd first heard him in was nearly 150 years old and creaked with age. Besides, having an orchestra, an opera company, and a dance company all performing there made for tight schedules and no room to grow.

Four years later, Gergiev once again brought his orchestra to Toronto. We didn't have to sponsor them this time. The banks were falling over themselves to connect their names to the Mariinsky's. As with all of their Toronto appearances, Jean and I would host a post-concert dinner party in our condo for Gergiev. That party wouldn't start until 11:00 p.m. and wouldn't get going until Gergiev turned up. It would generally end at two in the morning. Vodka flowed, cigars smoked. But I knew that all I'd feel the next day was tired.

As always, my job was to whisk Gergiev from his dressing room into his waiting limo and get him to our place as soon after the concert as possible. This time, as the car made its way through the December snow, I made small talk by asking him how that project for the new Mariinsky Theatre was coming along.

"Oh, it's terrible," he replied.

"Really, how so?"

"The architect."

"What's wrong with the architect?"

"He's French."

"Ah yes, of course."

I didn't know what he was talking about. What happened to the American architect?"

"I think ..." Gergiev said, looking out the window of the limo onto the snow-clogged streets, "I think I shall fire him tomorrow."

Now when a CEO say this, maybe it's a figure of speech. But when an all-powerful musical director says it, best pay attention. And when that person is a Russian who's rumoured to be the god-father to Vladimir Putin's children (and vice versa), this brings a whole new meaning to the idea of "fire." Indeed, Putin and Gergiev were comrades in their early careers, Putin joining the First Directorate of the KGB in St. Petersburg as Gergiev was becoming the very young assistant conductor of the Kirov Opera.

I told Gergiev in the car that one of our dinner guests was Jack Diamond, the architect who had designed the Four Seasons

Centre for the Performing Arts in downtown Toronto, an opera house that drew great critical acclaim and instant loyalty from its burgeoning opera and dance audiences, but most special acclaim from Diamond's client, Richard Bradshaw, the general director of the Canadian Opera Company, who was also a friend of Gergiev's.

When we arrived at our condo I made sure to seat Gergiev next to Jack Diamond, whom I didn't really know, and, anyway, I didn't have time to tell him about Gergiev's search for a new architect. In fact, only a month before I'd happened to recognize Jack Diamond across a crowded hotel ballroom at a fundraiser of some kind, I'd gone up to him and introduced myself, and asked if he'd like to have dinner with Valery Gergiev. Of course he would.

Our dining table seats twelve people. Across from Gergiev and Diamond sat Phil Lind and Jim Fleck, both veterans of these dinners. Fleck was strangely silent during most of the dinner. He's usually a commanding conversationalist. Maybe he was tired. It *was* one thirty in the morning. So I went over to him and said, "Jim, are you okay?"

"Fine. I'm just watching these two sharks circle each other."

I heard later that by nine that morning, a package from Diamond Schmitt Architects was at the concierge desk at the Four Seasons Hotel where Gergiev was staying.

Three months later, Diamond Schmitt were appointed the architects to design the New Mariinsky Theatre, across the canal from the Old Mariinsky Theatre.

Four years after that, in May of 2013, a gang of sixty-five "Gergiev Groupies" made our way to St. Petersburg for the opening of the first new opera house to be built in Russia since the czars.

The first person who walked out onstage was the man who had paid the €785 million bill for a complex that is four times the footprint of the Four Seasons Centre in Toronto.

Vladimir Putin.

And, to think, this odd and ongoing story all began because my distant father took me as a boy to orchestra concerts in Edmonton; because a strange Greek woman late one night in the Courtyard Café in Toronto told me I should become friends with her cousin; because Costa and I lived in a madhouse for three years together; because one day on a picnic in Amsterdam, Costa told us about his great new Russian conductor; because a year later we took up his crazy invitation to go to a summer music festival in St. Petersburg; and because we were so awestruck by this conductor that we put up money he didn't ask us for in order to hear him again — and, as it turned out, again, and again, and again.

That's one reason Costa was sitting at that table with the three other men at Jean Paul and Kate's wedding. The other was that he'd taken Jean Paul under his wing a few years before, when Jean Paul was job-hunting in London where Costa and his wife, Liz, by then lived.

Jean Paul stayed with them for two weeks as he went the rounds of the global banks and investment houses looking for an entry-level management job. But even though he'd done very well in commerce at the University of Toronto, that didn't quite translate into open doors the way graduating from Harvard and Stanford did. And in the evenings while Costa was with his artists in the concert halls of the world, Liz was home teaching Jean Paul about nutrition and how to cook. Costa and Jean Paul became friends, as well, independent of Jean and me, and likely in spite of Jean and me. He could talk about stuff that neither his father nor his stepfather could — and both Jean and I were grateful for that.

One thing Jean Paul didn't inherit from his mother was her sense of adventure. When he returned home, I asked him how he liked London. "It was okay, I guess. But the streets aren't straight like they are here."

There is that, I guess. I then asked him if he found London expensive.

"It's a killer."

I wondered what part of his trip was killing him. He had free room and board. He was attending opening nights at the opera. He was eating like a king.

"The subway fares," Jean Paul replied.

Ah, to be young and in London ...

I first met Dan O'Connor via email.

Nearly a hundred women had joined JeansMarines in 2002 to run the Marine Corps Marathon in Washington, D.C. We almost didn't go for fear of being shot by the Washington sniper. But he was caught the night before the morning we all left for the U.S. capital and a weekend that would change all our lives.

We'd arrived on Friday for the race on Sunday.

I'd arranged for us to have a reception at the Canadian Embassy in Washington on the Friday night. There would be a film crew with us doing a one-hour documentary on the story of how a hundred middle-aged women had decided to get off the couch and train for nine months for an athletic event none of them gave a thought to doing a year before. We'd have cocktails then we'd all go into the auditorium and Jean would speak. Then I, as the propagandist-in-chief, would speak, and one or two other JeansMarines would also speak.

What was missing here was someone who knew what they were talking about. Someone who knew about the U.S. Marine Corps and the Marine Corps Marathon.

So two months before we arrived, I called the race organizers and asked if it would be possible for them to send "an expert" to talk to us. Of course they could. They did this all the time because of so many charitable groups and first-timers doing the race. They said I'd get an email from someone in a few days. When that didn't happen, I called again and they assured me someone would be in touch. A week later, I received an email from Captain Dan O'Connor, USMC. Long afterward, Dan told me the reason for the delay.

They'd never received a request from a group made up entirely of foreign runners, and certainly never for an event to be held in a foreign embassy. They couldn't send just any Marine. It had to be an officer. And that officer had to be good.

Captain O'Connor and I went back and forth on the details of the event. I'd introduce him. Then he'd speak for ten minutes about the U.S. Marine Corps and its storied history, followed by a history of the Marine Corps Marathon, then he'd be happy to answer our questions. We agreed to meet up fifteen minutes before the reception.

Meanwhile, two days before we left, Jean was riding her bike, swerved to miss a car, hit the brakes, and fell head over heels over the handlebar. She cut her lip badly. Later that night, our family dentist, Dr. Bonnie Chandler, saw Jean in her office, cleaned her up, straightened out a couple of loose teeth, and sent us both home. But at the embassy Jean still bore the stiff upper lip of the bike accident.

Before I met Dan O'Connor, I tried to picture him. His resumé told me he'd been the head of the U.S. Marine Corps SWAT squad, a provost marshal (chief of police) at two Marine bases, a top pistol shot in the Marine Corps, and the head of the close-quarters battle school.

Tough. Very tough.

So I had this image of a tall, slim Marine with a ramrod salute.

He, too, had an image of me. I of course was a tall, slim marathoner.

When we actually met, it was all we could do not to laugh.

I'm five foot three and never slim.

Dan was easily six foot three and built like a hulking tank.

I introduced him to Jean and her swollen lip. Over the next hour, he shook hands with all hundred of the women who made up our first JeansMarines brigade. He seemed charmed by them ... these middle-aged non-American women whose values seemed so different from what we thought the U.S. Marines stood for.

But of course, we were wrong about that.

In the auditorium, I welcomed all of us to Canada's home in America, then introduced Captain O'Connor. With the documentary cameras rolling, he walked to the microphone and said, "On behalf of the President of the United States, the Commandant of the Marine Corps, and the Race Director, I would like to welcome you to Washington, D.C., and the 2002 Marine Corps Marathon."

Wow.

We all cheered. This was bigger than we thought.

He and I'd agreed that he would speak for ten minutes on the history of the Marine Corps and of the marathon.

He didn't do that.

His next words were: "The U.S. Marines are the toughest fighting force in the world. I've been a Marine for twenty-five years, so I've seen tough. I've seen courage under fire. But the toughest, most courageous person I know is ..."

"... my mom."

Huh?

"My father abandoned my mother, my two brothers, and me when I was three. We lived on welfare and food stamps, and my mom worked two and sometimes three jobs. She could have quit and just given in, but that's not what she's about. I see a lot of her qualities in all of you."

I looked around at all the women. They were stunned. Many, including Jean, started to choke up, their eyes red.

In a way that would happen over and over during our long relationship with Captain (and eventually Major) Dan O'Connor, he had us at hello.

That was on Friday night. On Saturday, we had our pre-race pasta dinner at a nearby hotel. The idea of bulking up on carbs before the big race may not help you run faster or farther the next day, but it's a marathon tradition the world over.

We ate early, in order to get to bed early and get some sleep before the big race on Sunday. As we streamed out of the hotel dining room into the lobby and then outside, we heard what sounded like a brass band. Indeed, it was: the U.S. Marine Corps brass quintet, standing outside the hotel to serenade us — JeansMarines.

Dan O'Connor wasn't there. But clearly he'd arranged this private concert for his Canadian women. And when they started playing "O Canada," the tears flowed and our voices broke as we belted out our national anthem played by the living, breathing symbol of America and its military might.

The concert done, we all walked back to our own hotel higher than kites and with absolutely zero chance of sleep.

Sunday was race day and Dan O'Connor was where he'd been for ten years, in charge of the race's finish line. In Washington that wasn't just a line crossing a street somewhere. It was at the Iwo Jima Memorial, with its fabled giant sculpture of six Marines raising the flag of victory at the Battle of Iwo Jima in the Japanese Volcano Islands in 1945, near the end of the American campaign in the Pacific in the Second World War. Like much of the U.S. Marines and of Washington, it is laden with symbolism. As a Canadian I felt a bit of a trespasser yet thrilled to share in their glory.

Marathons are inherently chaotic and finish lines especially. Runners are exhausted, exhilarated, in agony, in ecstasy. Quite a few are injured. Very occasionally, they'll die. Which is why nearly all big marathons have a first aid tent at the finish line, and why the

Marines had what looked to be a Level 4 Cardiac Unit in a huge tent. I learned later that they treat the entire race as a military exercise in crowd control and mass casualties.

At the end of most marathons, a volunteer hands you a medal, someone else gives you a foil blanket to keep you from chilling down, and then it's on to the pretzel and banana tables, and finally to the waiting area to meet your cheering family and friends. There's one big difference in the Marine Corps Marathon.

When you cross the finish line, a young Marine puts a medal around your neck and then gives you a hug. I would mention this to the women we were hoping to sign up for that year's Marine Corps — and remember, nearly all of them were feminists or ultrafeminists. But when I told them that a U.S. Marine was guaranteed to give them a hug if they finished the race, they turned to putty before my eyes.

The race starts early in the morning and the fastest runners cross the finish about two and a half hours later. But the vast majority of us finish much later, and the stragglers can take over six hours to do the course. Pretty much all of these original JeansMarines made it across the finish line in four to five hours. But when we were cheering our teammates across the finish, one of us wasn't crossing, Betty-Lou Durr. She was a nurse at Women's College Hospital where Jean delivered babies. Not in five hours, not in six, not in … it was beginning to get dark and chill.

If this marathon was like all the others, the organizers would close down the finish line after six and a half hours. Too dark. Too risky. But maybe she'd finished earlier and gone back to the hotel. Oh well … we all walked back, exhausted and triumphant, to our hotel to shower and get changed for our … victory dinner!

What a gathering of the gods that was. Here were a hundred women, a hundred *Canadian* women, plus a few good men, who no one gave a chance of finishing the Marine Corps Marathon, let alone even making it to the start line, when we all began training back in February. We all wore our medals. We were all bursting with pride. The speeches were clamorous. The cheers loud and long. Then Dan O'Connor rose. We'd invited him to our dinner because by then we'd adopted him. He got up and told us how we'd all shown the world what we're made of. Loud cheers. We were heroes. Louder cheers. We did what most people only dream of. Riotous cheers.

But there was one JeansMarine who deserved our special praise.

Who could that be? Jean had finished first among women in the fifty-to-fifty-five age group. But we didn't know that then.

It was Betty-Lou Durr. "Come on up, Betty-Lou. I have something to give you." Betty-Lou stood and limped to the where Dan O'Connor was standing. Then he told us her story.

At Mile 17 of the 26.2 mile race, she had pulled a muscle in her thigh. She went to a first aid tent where she was told it would be wise to stop and withdraw from the race. Not Betty-Lou. She shouldn't really run. So she walked. The more she walked, the slower she got. She was in real pain, but she wouldn't stop. A police motorcycle said she couldn't cross the bridge four miles from the finish because they had to open it to traffic. She moved off the road and onto the sidewalk.

Then an ambulance came up and told her they would drive her to the finish line.

No, thank you. She kept walking. They radioed ahead. There was a woman who likely wouldn't finish, but if she did, it would be after they closed down the finish line. Dan O'Connor asked what her bib number was. He checked her name and age and hometown. Toronto, Canada.

"Is she wearing a T-shirt that says JeansMarines?"

"Yes, sir, she is."

"We'll keep the finish open for her."

So Dan waited and waited until Betty-Lou, with a police escort, made her way painfully up the final hill at the Iwo Jima Memorial and crossed the finish line into Dan's waiting arms.

We know it happened this way because the film crew followed her all the way to the end, and that extraordinary finish is all in the documentary.

As is the final scene of our post-race dinner, when Dan pulled out a second finishers' medal and put this one around her neck, as well — making Betty-Lou the only person to win two medals in the 2002 Marine Corps Marathon on that glorious Sunday in November.

That badge of courage was a hallmark of JeansMarines and Dan O'Connor's role in it for the six years we existed. Dan O'Connor grew pretty quickly from a friend and mentor of every JeansMarine, into a close member of our own family. He's been there for us in the days of triumph and hours of despair.

In 2006, he retired from the Marines and worked for Homeland Security, then headed disaster security planning for FEMA, the Federal Emergency Management Agency.

He and his wife and daughters join us heli-hiking in the Rockies. He loves coming to Toronto because it — and we — are so different from what he deals with daily in America. He also loves playing "the big dumb Marine" with our many "liberal" friends. Little do they know they're about to tangle with a guy who's graduated from the Kennedy School at Harvard, twice.

But what is it they say about U.S. Marines?

No worse enemy. No better friend.

And all of this — his loyalty, his complexity, his patriotism — is why Dan O'Connor took the third place at our table for four at our son's wedding dinner.

* * *

The final seat at that table was occupied by a man so seemingly unlike Dan O'Connor that I thought all that would pass between them was awkward silence. I was thrilled to be proven wrong.

The Rev. Brent Hawkes.

His public claim to fame is that he performed the first legal same-sex marriage in the world. It took place in the church he was then the senior pastor of, the Metropolitan Community Church of Toronto.

My own religious life was normal for a private school kid whose school was modelled on the great "public" schools of England and their defining Victorian colonial traditions.

Trinity College School in Port Hope, Ontario, may be light years away from Eton and Harrow. But it seems the farther an institution gets from the mother ship, the more earnestly it tries to emulate it. Distance makes the heart grow stronger.

So for six school years, between 1962 and 1968, I went to church once a day and twice on Sunday. When I was fourteen, I was confirmed into the Anglican Church of Canada. My parents came from Edmonton for the ceremony. I joined the school choir and in my grade thirteen year was the head choirboy, singing the much sought-after solo at the Christmas carol service.

But none of this stuck with me. After I graduated from Trinity, I never thought of going to church. I loved singing the countless hymns I'd memorized. But as for believing in God, well …

My lack of faith all came to a strange head in 2011 when Michael Enright interviewed me on his CBC radio program, *Sunday Edition*. He'd asked me to come on and tell people what it was like to die. He'd read my piece in *Maclean's* about my death experience when my heart stopped after open-heart surgery. I told him that whatever I had to say would make bad radio because, in terms of drama, nothing happened. No angels lifted me up. My friends and loved ones didn't gather around me. Certainly my life didn't pass before my eyes.

I said to him that it was as if the two of us had gone to a movie together and I'd nodded off in the middle, then you nudged me and said, "Bob, wake up. You were dead for a bit there." I had no memory of my death whatsoever.

What I told Enright is that I wanted to come on to his show and talk about the depression that so often follows open-heart surgery. He agreed and I went into the studio to tape the show, which would be broadcast two weeks later.

Over my career, I've trained countless executives and authors on how to handle media interviews. But it seems when it came to me appearing on the media, I forgot to train myself — even to think what he might ask me.

So when Michael Enright said, "Tell me, Bob, do you believe in God?," I was struck dumb.

Thanks heavens for editing, which removed the long and awkward pause from the on-air version as I desperately tried to think of what to say.

Two weeks later, up at our cottage, we turned on CBC Radio to join a million Canadians in hearing Bob Ramsay's views on God.

"Well, Michael. I'd like to think of myself as a faithful atheist. I believe in the music of the church. I believe in its care for the sick and the old. I believe in its outreach programs. I just don't believe there's a God."

That was the God's truth and I thought it was quite a clever answer, as well, until two minutes later when I happened to be checking my email and into my inbox came the first of a flurry of emails from members of the religious right who objected to my claiming to be a faithful atheist.

I'm not the hardest person to find online. But two minutes? To hear my blasphemy, go online, find our website, find my email, then write an email telling me I would burn in hell, then hit *Send*?

The fact is, most people I know are faithful atheists. Jean was brought up in a stern Presbyterian farming household. She loves the old hymns, like "The Old Rugged Cross." But the only thing Sunday school in southern Ontario farm country seems to have bequeathed her is a huge sense of guilt. In 1999, when her youngest daughter, Ryan, turned eighteen, she practically begged Ryan to be christened by Brent Hawkes, even though she had displayed absolutely zero interest in anything religious. Ryan did it purely because Jean had confessed to her that she dreaded Ryan suddenly dying and being kept from heaven's door because she was unchristened.

Now that's guilt!

But I'm getting ahead of myself.

Brent was at the wedding dinner because he'd performed the service.

But he'd performed the service because he had reintroduced Jean and me to a community of faith where we could feel comfortable — uplifted, in fact. It began with that crazy Christmas Eve carol service at Roy Thomson Hall. It grew as we came to know Brent.

I fell in love with his articulation first, of course, while Jean fell in love with his steadiness. His sermons were masterworks of wit and connection.

He was also not afraid to be funny from the pulpit, a quality rarely heard from such lofty heights. We both loved Brent's civil activism, as well. Fighting for equality when you're gay is easier in Toronto than lots of other places in the world. But his insistent stubbornness in defining gay rights not as a sexual issue, but as a human rights issue, is what brought him to don a bulletproof vest to perform the first same-sex marriage, and to win the Order of Canada.

He often says, "There are many paths to God," and while I still don't believe there's an afterlife, I do know that Brent Hawkes's words will give me much-needed comfort at the end of my life. I hope it will be like falling asleep in the movies and not having someone nudge me awake to say, "Hey, you were dead," because this time I really will be. One can only hope.

Jean has a much more informed view on death and dying, of course, since at least once a week she is not only at her patient's bed-side as they die; she is the instrument of their death. Let's not mince words here: she kills them. More on this in the final chapter.

We're still enjoying the four-guys wedding-dinner table. The con-versation was animated, respectful, and open-ended. I don't know why I expected anything less. We all knew how to behave. To some degree, all of us talked for a living.

Three of us were enormous extroverts and Dan O'Connor was just finding his way as a big thinker who loved to tease my white-wine liberal friends.

Maybe it was because we'd all reached an age when our shared abiding philosophy was "whatever gets you through the night." Or because we were all old enough that life had beaten us up and we knew that rigid orthodoxies often kept us from being who we really wanted to be. Or because we were all just trying to make the second half of our lives happier than the first may have been.

I told the story of how Jean Paul had been not overly pro-gay as a teenager, in the way we think a high school football player would be. But when his younger sister, Ryan, came out, it didn't take long for him to become her staunchest defender.

Costa I knew viewed gays as about as aberrant as people who are left-handed.

Dan O'Connor was a role model for hundreds, if not thousands of young men in one of the most homophobic organizations in America: the U.S. Marines. While he never said a peep one way or the other about what he thought of gay Marines, I got a sense his views changed over the years. They usually do when you work in close quarters with people whom tradition has taught you to dislike and avoid, and when that person can save your life. It also turned out that one of the ministers in Brent's church was a former U.S. Marine, a woman who left the Marines, changed her sexual preference, became a minister, moved to Canada, and ended up at MCC Toronto. That, too, made for a quick and real bond between Brent and Dan.

At the start of the dinner, I was worried about everyone's getting along, even though I'd put the four of us together. By dessert, long after the conversation had moved from polite chit-chat into deep connection, I realized just how insistent my unconscious was in forcing people together. It was as if I believe (and I do) that if I'm close to Dan and I'm close to Brent, then Dan and Brent not only will be close to each other, but that I must forge that closeness by bringing them together. The lovely thing is that, in nearly all cases, this clunky logic works.

In fact, in my zeal to connect people I will sometimes skip the preliminaries and go directly to the climax. I may be at a reception, a concert, even a movie and spot two people who I know share a great love for, let's say John le Carré, or kayaking, or kidney transplants. I will cross the room and grab one of them and say, "Follow me. It's important." They reluctantly do. I'll drag them over to meet another friend, and sometimes not even a friend, but just someone I met ten minutes earlier, and I'll say, "You two read Jared Diamond and are lawyers. You should talk." I'll then introduce them and leave. True, they'll stand there a little gobsmacked, but they'll soon start connecting via the little information they have about each other. Lawyers and Jared Diamond. More often than not, those two slim vectors will turn into a deep web.

Once, I ran into a woman I vaguely knew from business at a board of trade lunch. She was in her early sixties and had cut her hair almost to her scalp.

"Wow," I said. "That's an amazing haircut."

"Brain tumour."

"Pardon me?"

"I had a brain tumour, so the surgeons had to shave my head."

"Oh ..."

But rather than leave it at that, I said, "Do you know Jane Somerville? She has a brain tumour, and they shaved her head, too. You should get together."

Yup. That bad.

Yes, part of this is an age-and-stage thing. Part of it is that, like pretty much everyone's, my friends share my values. But part of it also is that they'd better reach for a deeper connection.

I don't think I have a passion for deep connection with people. I think I have an addiction for deep connection. Did it start when I was both starved for affection and then overwhelmed by it when I was growing up? Who knows? At this stage, it doesn't really matter.

What matters is that I've become good at something I love doing, and the more I know people and the more people I know, the deeper my own connections get.

Like any self-respecting addict, I can get too easily drunk, even on people and bringing them together. The price of my addiction is exhaustion at some level and the fear of not being able to stop.

While Jean can be very social, she's also able to operate pretty much on her own steam. She loves her patients. She lives the torments and delights they go through. But she's much more private than I am and is happy to remain so.

The fact is, most nights Jean and I are at home. We'll have dinner and then bury our heads in our computers: me catching up on the day's emails and writing whatever short assignment that I can get done before I start to mentally shut down, Jean filling out forms and writing notes for her patients who want medically assisted death — a hard, exacting protocol that can involve the patient's families, their hospital, and even the coroner, who pronounces on the validity of every medically assisted death in Ontario. Best to get an opinion in advance, Jean's learned. In this field of medicine, getting one afterward has a different set of consequences.

We actually follow this routine most nights, despite my reputation for always been out at concerts and parties.

One night in 2019, Jean looked up from her computer and said, "You know what, honey. We're losing touch with people."

I looked up.

"What did you say?"

She repeated her claim. She'll occasionally do this, commenting out of the blue on what, in this case, was clearly something she'd just read online.

"We're losing touch?"

That was preposterous. Was she dementing?

"Yes, we're losing touch with people, and especially young people. We only know old people."

"I don't really think that's true, honey."

Where was she going with this crazy notion?

"Who do we know who's under forty?"

"Uh … our grandkids?"

She was not amused.

"So why don't you have a dinner party just for young people?"

By "you," she meant "we."

Like what?

"Well, we have dinner all the time for your speakers. But the focus is always on them. Why don't we invite ten young people to our condo for dinner and the focus will be on them?"

And thus was born the Killer Young People's Dinners.

We've had five KYPDs over the past year. They were all wonderful in a strange and exhilarating way. We learned that men and women between thirty and forty need no lessons from us in making connections, except our impetus to bring them together. They also drink much more than friends our age.

Best of all, we have fifty new friends we never had before. With lots of invitations to enter their world that's just not open to people of our age and stage. And a heads-up on how much they're like their hosts who are thirty to forty years older than they are — in the eternals like making your way in the world, being accepted, having kids, paying the rent, etc.

But also, and much more important, we learned how very different these young people are, as well — in rejecting the values that drove us so incessantly when we were that age, like buying a home, driving a car, polluting the environment, and believing that tomorrow would always be better than today.

As James Watson, the co-discoverer of DNA, said when he was eighty-five, "I'm often asked how to stay young at heart. I reply: 'Avoid old people, at all costs.'"

24 Meet Your Surgeons

Most Friday nights, winter and summer, we head the two hours north to Georgian Bay, where we spend the weekend alone together. We're lucky to have a cottage, lucky that Jean chose to take the plot of land instead of the RRSPs in negotiating her first husband's divorce, very lucky to have a cottage to flee to when Covid-19 hit.

Friends will say, "You must have such great parties up north!" Actually, we never have parties up north. The only people we invite up there are our kids and grandkids. Otherwise, our heads would explode from the sheer intensity of life in the city.

Do we unplug from the internet? Well, no. That's an addiction neither of us can seem to beat. What we mainly do is go to our corners and work. Or sit in front of the fireplace and read. Or Jean heads to the garage, which doubles as a woodworking shop, and spends the weekend making a bowl that she proudly shows off Sunday night when she's done.

Jean got the property for the cottage in 1989. It sat there for four years before we could afford to build on it, and it's since been done over three times into a family compound on Thunder Beach, directly across from Christian Island, made famous in the Gordon Lightfoot song of the same name.

And as we get older, we use the cottage as a base camp for extended adventures, like sixty-mile bike rides through the rolling hills of Tiny Township, so named after a pet dog of the wife of an early lieutenant-governor of Upper Canada.

Or like overnight kayak trips where we'll pack up our kayaks on a Friday and head as far north to Parry Sound as we can get before putting in on a convenient rock that's big enough to accommodate our tent for one or two nights before we head back Sunday afternoon. In fact, it was this impulse, plus the purchase of two sea kayaks, that got us both into kayaking — another long-distance endurance sport we've become attracted to. As with our first marathon, we were largely self-taught. That education included some pretty windy days caught in Georgian Bay storms; and being picked up by the Coast Guard who took one look at us, determined we were too old to paddle in from the Brébeuf Island Lighthouse, and promptly loaded us and our kayaks into their four-hundred-horse-power Zodiac and gave us a rocket-like lift into Penetanguishene.

But kayaking on Georgian Bay also gave us the impulse to go farther, risk more, take on the world. So it was on a beautiful September day in 2019 that we circumnavigated Manhattan — one kayak, one island, thirty-one miles, eleven hours.

Georgian Bay had been a snap compared to Manhattan. Both can have dreadful winds and Georgian Bay weather is notoriously skittish: dead calm one minute and a raging sea the next. But New York has three things not even the worst days of Georgian Bay can throw at a kayaker. It has tides, currents, and traffic — hundreds and hundreds of boats, all intent, it seemed, on swamping us. Oh, and it also has downwash from helicopters landing on the heliport in the East River without much regard for tiny kayaks in the water below.

We had a guide with us because, as the Manhattan Kayak Club's website says, "The Atlantic Ocean floods into and ebbs out from Hudson River several times daily. The water will literally sweep away any untrained kayakers."

Because of the tides, we couldn't start earlier than eleven in the morning. But the surprise benefit was that, in the final leg of the trip, as we turned left out of the Harlem River and headed south from 218th Street down the Hudson River to our endpoint at 44th Street, by the USS *Intrepid*, we had the sunset on our right, the stars above us, and downriver, the lights of Manhattan as we crossed under the George Washington Bridge in full moonlight.

When we had dinner near our hotel at eleven o'clock that night, the fried chicken, french fries, and full-cheese onion soup tasted triumphant.

We've had a lot of once-in-a-lifetime adventures together, often the same ones more than once. But this is one we agreed we'd not try a second time. At age seventy (me) and seventy-seven (Jean), it was best to avoid tempting fate.

Fate had tempted us — shockingly — one winter Saturday on Georgian Bay the year before. The alarm went off and we grunted awake. Jean's plan had been to run fifteen miles in the snowdrifts, her long training run for the Boston Marathon, which was two months off. My eyes were opening and closing and I saw Jean get out of bed. Then she disappeared.

"Honey?"

Where did she go? It was only five seconds since I saw her last.

"Jean?" I lifted myself up. She was on the floor by her side of the bed doubled over in pain.

"Honey, what's wrong?!"

She was in agony, holding her stomach.

I leapt out of the bed, grabbed her arm to hold her steady…

"Don't touch me!" she screamed. "The pain!"

"Shall I call 9-1-1?"

"Yes!"

I didn't know what was going on, but I knew this was potentially deadly. Jean can endure all kinds of pain. So for her to scream for the ambulance … Also, we were twenty minutes in the best of weather from the ambulance in Midland. I prayed that the road had been ploughed. I knew our driveway hadn't, and our cottage was at the bottom of a long, sloping hill down to the beach. So there was a good chance the ambulance could get down to us, but not get back up.

Jean was groaning in agony on the floor. In the half-hour it took for the ambulance to arrive, I was helpless to … well, do anything really. I couldn't carry her downstairs to our car. She couldn't take the pain.

When the paramedics arrived, they called in to get approval to give Jean morphine on the spot. They then had to get a special chair, the kind usually reserved for taking 450-pound patients out a window, to get Jean out of the bedroom, down the stairs, and into the ambulance.

And now the real test. Could it get back up the driveway.

It did, and I closed the cottage, hopped in the car, and followed the ambulance to Georgian Bay General Hospital in Midland.

The emerg doctor gave her more morphine, did an X-ray, and strongly suggested she get to Toronto and her "home hospital." So we drove home very *very* slowly, in order not to aggravate Jean's pain. When we arrived, Jean went right to bed, and called her doctor, Mary Rubino, only when she woke up that night. Mary said that if the pain got worse during the night, to go immediately to the Mount Sinai Hospital Emergency Department. If it didn't, to get some sleep and go when she woke up in the morning. Jean slept through the night, no doubt aided by the morphine, but the pain was rising, so we headed to Mount Sinai Emerg.

Flash forward to later that afternoon. She's got a twisted bowel and the ER doc says, in a chatty tone, "I think we're going to want to operate on that in the next hour or so."

I missed what he meant.

"The good news is," he told Jean, who was lying on a gurney in a hallway, "our on-call surgical team is actually in the hospital now. I'll bring them over in a few minutes to discuss the procedure and then we'll take you up to the operating room."

Again, he was so calm I missed what he was really saying: This was emergency surgery. It was life-or-death.

Five minutes later, I spotted the ER doc winding his way through the ER hallway with three women in tow. They were all wearing hijabs.

He came up to Jean's gurney.

"Dr. Marmoreo, this is your surgical team."

My eyes opened wide.

Isn't Mount Sinai the Jewish hospital? I thought.

It's Sunday night. This is the D-Team, and they're going to operate on my wife. No way.

"This is your anaesthetist, Dr. Soandso," the ER doc began. I couldn't make out any of their names. "This is Dr. Soandso, a member of our surgical team," introducing a woman in her early thirties.

"And this is Dr. Soandso, the head of emergency surgery." She was possibly forty.

They then talked for ten minutes, doctors to doctor, in words I could barely understand. But I was terrified.

They all left and soon an orderly came to wheel Jean into the operating room. I was with her as we rode the elevator up. We held hands and Jean said to me, "Honey, I have great faith in that head surgeon. Think what she's had to go through to get where she is."

And Jean was right. The surgery was a success, as was Jean's recovery, though our entire family had to work to keep Jean from starting to train for the Boston Marathon sooner than medically advisable. At times, dealing with Jean's determination is like trying to control a four-year-old. I used to think, why even try? But then, when it comes to fate and surgery, life and death re-enter the picture.

That picture was worth looking at again. We were up north in the middle of winter. Our cottage was on a dead-end road, hard to get in and out of. The nearest hospital was twelve miles away.

Something out of the blue had nearly struck Jean ... dead, actually. If we'd been truly off the grid, she would be gone. And she's not the one with the risky prognosis. I'm the one who's going to stroke out in a kayak miles from shore, or fall over skiing in the woods and not be heard from until spring.

The next month, I installed video cameras inside and outside our cottage and in our garage up there where Jean has her woodworking shop. There's a camera and an alarm in our cottage basement, as well. If one of us is alone up north — or the other is out on a five-hour run or bike ride — and falls down the stairs, or in Jean's case, cuts off her finger on the lathe in the garage, then what ...?

These technologies can cut our risk a bit, I think, though Jean thinks it's just a waste of money.

But this entire incident that began with Jean falling out of bed taught me that we're now in the highest-risk zone of them all.

Old age.

25   In the Departure Lounge

B ette Davis said, "Old age is no place for sissies." But now that I'm in my seventies I still hope it's a place for deniers.

True, it's hard to refute reality when reading obits becomes an obsession and friends drop dead left and right.

But I remember the times I was close to death before — during drug binges and after heart surgery. I don't recall feeling any particular rage to live; rather, a wave of enormous passivity, as easy as closing my eyes and going to sleep, covered and comforted me.

Yet how could someone so alive feel this way about death?

Because I think my high anxiety and fetal sleeps are the two-sided masks for the denial that's both served me and stunted me all the days of my life. When my time really comes to depart for good, I'm certain I'll be fighting like hell to stay. I will be terrified, angry, mortified. We hear that many people are at peace when they die. Resigned and calm, they await oblivion. Not for me. Having been often saved from death throughout my life, I will breathe my last hoping that I'll be passed over again.

I guess this is the ultimate in magical thinking, the childhood fantasy that has me landing on my left foot at the top of stairways in order to stave off disaster. I can still glance at a set of stairs in a subway station and know what foot I must take my first step on in order to reach the final stair at the top on my left foot. You laugh.

But you do not understand just what a precious skill this is, how often it has saved my plane from crashing and my heart from breaking.

"It is common in very young children."

True, that. But like so much of my psyche (which was built to defend against all enemies, foreign and domestic), while the threats have long ago vanished, the defences are still there, hollowed cannons from unfought wars.

As I learned from my drug addiction, denial is a chameleon. Mine doesn't say, "You aren't sick … that lump is nothing … you don't need to see a doctor." Mine says, "You need to test everything. If you don't, you will die from not paying attention and you will deserve to."

When I was in university, I came across a sentence from Robert Penn Warren's *All the King's Men*, his florid retelling of the life of Huey Long, Louisiana's utterly corrupt governor of the 1930s. Warren's style suited the man — and hooked me forever. I quickly memorized this Very Long Thought and quote it now to friends whose arch looks ask, "Whatever does that mean?"

The end of man is knowledge, but there is one thing he can't know. He can't know whether knowledge will save him or kill him. He will be killed, all right, but he can't know whether he is killed because of the knowledge which he has got or because of the knowledge which he hasn't got and which if he had it, would save him.

They should tape that to the inside of every MRI machine.

But die I most certainly will. The bank believes I'll do that when I'm ninety, a number they claim is actuarially sound. But they told me that in 2011, the year I did die the first time. I think they did it to cheer me up and sell me catastrophic illness insurance.

No, the much better odds are that I'll stroke out. That's why I take blood-thinner pills every day. Or have another heart event (and why I have a pacemaker). Or maybe my bladder cancer will recur. I do know that I'm virtually uninsurable when it comes to anything involving heart or cancer, which will kill two out of three North American men in their seventies.

But my secret hope is that I'll fall off a mountain with Jean.

This is not a fantasy at all. Given the pace of how the two of us attack the world and the dangerous places we do it, dying accidentally is a very real prospect.

That implies violently, which suggests agonizing pain. Which makes me hope for a quick end to it all. Oh ... and a heroic one, too, of course. I'm with Malcolm, who says in *Macbeth*, "Nothing in his life became him like the leaving it." You can't live meaningfully without hoping to die that way, too.

Jean takes a different view, one informed not just by reality, but by greeting death face to face almost every day.

For doctors, death isn't some black-hooded stranger.

But in 2016, Jean gave up delivering babies to take up a new medical subspecialty. She still practises family medicine in the clinic three days a week.

But, on Tuesdays and Thursdays, she now helps very sick, very old, very agonized people hasten their deaths. She began doing something that until 2016 was completely illegal and was treated as manslaughter: she became an assisted-suicide doctor.

This has changed her life — and mine, too.

She became a MAiD doctor — providing Medical Assistance in Dying — five years ago at age seventy-four in order to take care of her patients from cradle to heaven.

The length of that doctor-patient relationship, not to mention its intensity and its understanding of the people who are most important to her patients, created for Jean the possibility of an extraordinarily deep relationship.

Yet, at the very time the patient needs the skills and compassion of their family doctor most, that doctor is too often cut out of the relationship, reduced to an outsider looking in on the oncologists, cardiologists, and gerontologists who take charge of the relationship with their patients.

So she wanted back in.

She also knew that too many of her patients died terrible deaths, in excruciating pain. If the laws changed so these deaths didn't have to be so awful, all the more reason that she would raise her hand to train for a new medical specialty that no one had any expertise in because no one's done it before.

Helping patients die comes with all kinds of thorny moral, ethical, legal, and family issues. Don't all doctors take an oath to do no harm? What if some of the adult children are in favour of mom ending it all, and some are against — and they're all your patients? What if a patient in their twenties, having been approved for medical assistance in death because he has ALS, insists that he have a gender change because he wants to die as a woman?

For me, these are the subjects of dinnertime conversation as she recounts the events of her day.

Over the years, I've become inured to the stresses she faces daily, the stress she puts on herself. This is true for marathon training in blinding snowstorms up north. Or dealing with dozens and dozens of patients who pour in and out of her examining room every day. Or learning to be an expert woodworker by enrolling in a course for … expert woodworkers.

One of the things I love most about this woman is her "Let's get on with it" attitude toward everything — especially when that thing doesn't exist.

She isn't much interested in talking about it; much more in putting her head down and doing it.

Given her years of experience doing just this, I assume that she's strong enough to endure anything. But one day when I was telling a lawyer-friend about Jean's new specialty, he asked, "What kind of help is she getting?"

"Help? For what?"

"For all the stress."

"The stress?"

He looked askance at me, not quite believing I could be so unaware just how inherently stressful it is to end someone's life.

"Of course. Police and EMS people not only have access to therapy; they're ordered to talk to someone."

"Hmm … right." So that night I asked Jean if the people doing MAiD could talk to anyone afterward.

"You mean the nurses?" she asked.

"Well, yes, the nurses for sure, but also the doctors." I looked deeply into her eyes.

"I guess … maybe some of the young doctors …"

"No, honey, I mean YOU!"

"Me? Oh heavens, I'm an old dog."

I didn't say any more because I knew that if I pushed, Jean would simply pooh-pooh the idea. Forget that she tells people every day how and where to get professional help for stress and trauma. When it comes to her, well, the rules don't apply. Or rather, the rule seems to be: do as I say, not as I do.

It's easy to fall in line with that view, that Jean's just in denial about the psychological toll that inducing someone's death brings on her, and in many ways I'm sure it's right. But stress reduction takes many different and odd forms.

I discovered Jean's one day when I phoned her midafternoon to leave a message on her mobile's voice mail. Jean never answers her phone directly. So I was a bit surprised when she picked up. I gave her the message and asked, "Where are you?"

"Oh, I'm just walking down Yonge Street."

Jean Marmoreo does not just walk down Yonge Street in the afternoon, and it struck me as slightly odd.

But when the same thing happened two weeks later, I knew something else was at play, which I confirmed by remembering she had performed MAiD procedures on both of those days. The penny dropped. After each procedure, Jean goes for a walk along the busiest street in the country where there are all kinds of people and places ... and life.

26 A Stroke of Bad Luck

For two or three weeks a year, Jean and I don't see each other. When we're apart, I'm relieved; and even though I've never asked, I'm sure she is, too. This relief isn't for the usual reasons couples are happier apart than together; it's that life gets intense and stays that way when we're with each other. Even when we're alone together, in our separate corners.

Ten years ago, Jean decided to take up woodworking, something she was introduced to when she was a camp doctor at Glen Bernard Camp, an all-girls summer camp in Northern Ontario. Joc Palm, the camp's owner and director, and an active feminist before most of us knew that word, believed that teenaged girls should have the same right to learn "shop" that boys do. So she built a fully kitted-out woodworking shop for the girls to get their hands dirty working with wood. It turns out that being a camp doctor is not exactly Médecins Sans Frontières. The worst ailment seems to be homesickness. So Jean had plenty of time during the day to wander over to the shop and try her hand at basic woodworking.

Then one night at a dinner party in Toronto, Jean met Michael Fortune, the woodworking master whose maple-inlaid dining table graces Rideau Hall. The two of them talked about medical things, as often happens when Jean meets someone new at a dinner. Even though she knew that Michael is one of the world's most respected woodworkers, she would never think to ask the obvious question, which I had to do for her: "Do you hold woodworking classes?"

"Yes, I do. But they're not in Toronto; they're in Indianapolis."

"Oh." That was too bad.

"But Jean," said Fortune, "why don't you come up to my studio in Lakefield some weekend and we'll build a table together?"

Clearly, this is not an invitation he issues lightly. He had no idea of her skills with wood. But he had a hunch he wouldn't be wasting his time on an inept newbie.

Jean's view was a kind of grateful terror, the way you'd feel if Karen Kain asked you to spend a weekend dancing with her after you'd said you like dancing.

So one summer's day, Jean and I drove to Michael Fortune's woodworking studio in a converted barn off a country road northeast of Toronto. I dropped her off at noon on Saturday and picked her up on Sunday evening.

When Jean emerged triumphant with a small coffee table that she and Michael had "made" together, she was beaming. Michael Fortune looked pretty happy, too, saying, "She's got a good eye, but I've never seen anyone focus so well or work so hard."

Fortune teaches at something called the Marc Adams School of Woodworking, which is off a country road south of Indianapolis. Apparently, it's the world capital of woodworking, with hundreds of students pouring through every year. So Jean goes there for a week each spring and fall to learn things like Making Segmented Baskets and Making a Morris Chair.

She's still one of the few women there. But the growing cohort is retired surgeons who want to keep their hand-to-eye skills in shape. She's also a star student. And, as happens when someone gets very good, very fast, they go very deep, too. This always seems to include buying the gear to do the thing you're learning to do even better, faster, and deeper. I know nothing about woodworking tools beyond what I see on the shelves of Canadian Tire. But this world is akin to sailing or golf or marathoning. (You think running far takes a T-shirt and shorts and a pair of shoes? Ha!) It can get very expensive almost instantly. As with so much in life, it's all about the gear.

When Jean called at the end of her first week's session to say that she'd bought a couple of tools that she wanted to bring home on the plane, I asked if they were heavy.

"Not really. But they may not let them on the plane. They're chisels."

"Couldn't you buy them in Toronto when you get back?"

"Oh no. They're precision chisels."

Precision chisels? "Are they made in Germany or something?" I was serious.

"Germany? Heavens no," Jean replied, the way you would if I asked if your new car was an import from Communist Poland. "They're from Japan."

Ah yes, I thought. *You don't want that cheap junk from Germany. You want …*

"And what did you pay for them, dear?"

"A thousand dollars."

"A thousand dollars ... for a chisel?"

"Not for one; it's for two."

"Oh, whew, for a second there, I thought you were spending too much on tools."

Over the years I've learned not to ask such questions. It only makes her dig in her heels. Needless to say, the garage at our cottage up north has been turned into a woodshop worthy of Joc Palm's original training ground at Glen Bernard Camp, where Jean spends endless hours alone — when we're together.

On a Sunday morning last May, I picked Jean up at the airport from her Indianapolis flight and her latest week at woodworking school. The plan was to go straight to the cottage. So I packed for the cottage, dragging down my backpack, plus food and some books, to the car in our garage underneath our condo at Pape and Danforth in Toronto. As usual, I decided to take everything in one giant load. When I got to the car in the basement, it was all I could do to hold on to it all. But then I dropped my car keys, which meant putting everything on the garage floor, then opening the car and putting it all in the car.

I did that and now, with only my keys in my hand, went to open the front door of the car. But my keys fell out of my hand again. Odd. I bent down to pick them up and noticed that three of my fingers were curled into my palm. Only my thumb and first finger worked.

I'm having a stroke.

That was my first thought. My first action was to get in the car and drive. Don't just stand there and let fate have its way. Do something! Besides, my last health scare had happened in a basement, as well, in the Hilton Hotel eight years before. I also didn't know if my mobile worked in this garage. The reality was, fear, denial, self-preservation, and the need to stay calm were all fighting in my head. Naturally, fear won. So I got in the car and sped out of the garage, headed to either Toronto International Airport to pick up Jean — or to the Emergency Department at Toronto General Hospital.

I clutched the wheel with both hands. Those three fingers in my left hand were still useless. I tried to deny this, of course, deny what was right in front of my eyes. This was easy to do; I didn't feel any pain. Nothing else was amiss.

But gradually, as I drove closer to both the hospital and the airport, my head cleared and I was able to take stock. If this was a stroke, I'd better drive in the slow lane when I was on the expressway, the right lane so the car could rub into the guardrail and not crash into another car. As the turnoff for the hospital loomed ahead, I decided I'd rather have a stroke in the presence of my wife than in a hospital and have her not know where I was. So I drove on by, careful not to speed or to drive in anything but the right-hand lane.

I also hyperdiagnosed myself, checking incessantly that my eyesight was fine, my chin wasn't numb, and all of my other appendages were working.

I made it to the airport, parked at Terminal One, and got out. I noticed that I had a little feeling now in my fingers. Not much. At least it hadn't got worse. I was early to meet Jean's flight, so I got a coffee and waited.

I took the coffee in my left hand, the one whose fingers didn't work. I did this to prove that I was all right. So when I almost dropped the cup and had to quickly move my right hand in place to secure it, I thought just how important it was for me to face up to catastrophe by denying its existence. Drugs? I'm fine. Really. Desperate for love? No, not me. And now the stroke that will kill me, the stroke that Jean had predicted? It's gone. Magically cured. Never happened. I'm fine.

Jean came through the gate, saw me, and waved. We hugged. "How was it?" I asked. "Wonderful. I've got some wonderful bowls to show you. And some new tools, of course." That line had become a standing joke.

"Come over and sit down, honey. I need to show you something."

I told her what happened. She looked at my hand, then closely into my eyes, and started asking me the questions any nurse would ask in Emerg. I touched my fingers to my nose. Looked left, right, up, down. I also said my hand seemed to be getting less limp than in the garage at home.

"Well, dear, I think we'd better go to Toronto General. I'll call the kids and tell them we'll be late getting to the cottage."

So, an hour later, exactly as I'd done eight years earlier, I walked into Toronto General Emerg and said to the woman at the desk, "I'm having a stroke."

I long ago learned the incredible power of those words. They can get you to the front of the line at any hospital in Canada. The nurses didn't need to look at my health records to whisk me in pronto and do a stroke "workup" on me.

After an hour of testing, I noticed that my hand was restored to near normal, and I told the doctor that.

My diagnosis was that it was some kind of phantom incident, and now that things were back to normal, we can all forget it even happened, if indeed it did happen.

Her diagnosis was different.

"We can't be sure. But I'm almost certain you've had a TIA."

Jean had mentioned those three letters as she drove me to the hospital.

"A TIA is a mini-stroke, a Transient Ischemic Attack. It happens when there's a temporary lack of blood-flow to your brain. So it causes stroke-like symptoms like what's happened with your hand. But they usually resolve within twenty-four hours, and your hand is almost back to normal."

"So I had a stroke."

"Well, yes and no, though the risk of having a stroke is much higher for people who have a TIA. One in three will go on to have a full-blown stroke within a year."

Then she smiled briskly.

"But I wouldn't worry too much about it; you're on Coumadin."

Coumadin is the blood-thinning drug I've taken every day since 2011 to … well, to keep me from having a stroke. But it seems Coumadin didn't keep me from having a mini-stroke — and I said so.

"What we'll do, Mr. Ramsay, is send you to the Stroke Clinic and see what they say. It's Sunday today so they're not open. But we'll send the referral now and I'm sure you'll be hearing from them soon." Big smile. Jean was smiling, too.

Shouldn't they be frowning? I was.

We left the hospital and Jean said, "You want to drive?" I always drive when we're together.

"No, I don't."

"I'm happy to," Jean said, taking the keys. "But you shouldn't worry. You're on Coumadin."

We made our way to the cottage. By lunchtime, my hand was back to normal. I decided not to go for a long kayak ride on Georgian Bay, nor to go mountain biking up the escarpment behind our place. I spent that afternoon wondering when the next attack would happen. Clearly, whatever sense of security I enjoyed around my heart and my life had been punctured. Danger, quite deadly danger, had simply broken through all my defences and said, "I'm coming for you and there's nothing you can do about it."

This was not like my cancer. I hadn't girded myself against that the way I did a stroke or heart attack. For them, I was ready with blood thinners, an exemplary diet, exercise, pills to control my blood pressure and cholesterol — and of course, Coumadin.

The Stroke Clinic didn't call me that next week. What they did was send me a letter that arrived the week after telling me I had an appointment three weeks later. Who sends urgent appointment notices by mail? Jean took a different view: "I guess they saw your scans and concluded you're not at that much risk."

So, five weeks after my fingers went limp, I sat in front of the cardiac interventionist at the Toronto Western Hospital Stroke Clinic. She went through all my results and showed me where the blockage had happened. It was in my neck. You could see the tiny stain on the black-and-white image.

I asked if anything could be done to reduce the risk of it happening again. She said they could open my neck to clear the carotid artery, but the operation was risky and the artery wasn't really that blocked. Besides, she said, flashing a big smile, "You're on Coumadin!"

When I told Jean later that day what the specialist had said, she nodded and said, "Of course."

"So … what should I do?"

"Do? Nothing. There is nothing *to* do."

Aside from worrying incessantly about when, where, and how the next attack will come, then turning that worry into a finely polished bad dream of having that stroke and not being able to speak or write, let alone wipe my bum, and of course not being able to ask for doctor-assisted death because I'm not of sound mind or body, and not being able to take my own life, so I'm doomed to spend years, if not decades bedridden and waiting to die … aside from *that*, Jean's right.

There's nothing to do, but to carry on, knowing that every day grows more precious and more risky at the same time.

That was on May 22, 2019.

If you're reading this book, it's past June 2021 and I have every hope it hasn't been published posthumously.

27 Covid-19 Changes It All

Friday, March 13, 2020, was the day Toronto and much of Canada officially shut down. Offices, plants, and medical offices closed. Kids came home from school and daycare. Our Foodland store was already out of hand sanitizer and flour, and the scramble for masks was on.

That night, Jean and I drove two hours north to our cottage on Georgian Bay. We planned to stay there, on our water lot west of Penetanguishene, for a couple of weeks to hide out from the pandemic and see what the future held. That couple of weeks turned out to be over a year, and during that strange time we reconfigured our lives for a very different future.

Back in 2003, Jean had been a SARS doctor at Women's College Hospital, and she wanted to join her medical partners this time around, helping in the coronavirus clinics that were quickly popping up across the city. But her colleagues insisted she stay away. She was seventy-seven, and one thing that became clear very early on was the coronavirus's hunger for attacking old people. Jean sulked about this for a few days until she spoke with a friend who was an emergency room physician at St. Michael's Hospital in downtown Toronto. She, too, had been told by her fellow doctors to stay away — and she was fifty-five.

I had to remind myself that at seventy I, too, was old, no matter how young and unfrail we were compared to other people our age. So over a few days of bingeing on news reports, I moved from being blithely dismissive that our age put us in the path of the pandemic, to being completely certain that if we didn't scrub our counters twice daily with Clorox, even though no other humans were within hundreds of yards of us, we would both die. And not just die, but die gasping for breath, all alone. What could be worse?

While we'd had our cottage for thirty years, we'd never been there for more than a weekend when winter turns to spring. In mid-March it wasn't all babbling brooks and budding trees. That took a couple more months. The weather was as grey and dreary as we were.

As for work, Jean immediately moved to doing her family practice online. This was much easier said than done. Cottage-country Wi-Fi was as wobbly as our mobile phone coverage. We were among the thousands of households for whom secure Wi-Fi meant the difference between earning a living and not. It got solved for us only two months later after we switched phone carriers and got a new router, and that only happened after dozens of dropped calls and failed Zoom meetings, and having to go outside to make a phone call on a Monday, and then find a "live" room inside to make the same call on Tuesday.

Meanwhile, in the period of single week in March, I lost 90 percent of my business.

RamsayTravels hosts group travel for people who don't do group travel. RamsayTalks produces live speaker events with some of the world's leading thinkers. Ramsay Inc. makes most of its money by writing CEO speeches and offering writing and presentation courses — live. All of that ... the travel, the talks, the speeches, and courses ... gone.

I spent March scrambling to either postpone the travel and speaker events, or cancel them outright. My business manager of forty years, Joan Fischer, was a godsend, a role she's filled at pretty much every crisis point in my life. Together, we worked with the hotels and travel agents to move things into 2021 without paying huge financial penalties. As with millions of companies around the world, our new corporate mission was to preserve cash — at all costs.

I'd gone broke before due to drug addiction and I didn't relish the idea of doing that again, especially with Jean determined to retire at the end of the year. Our bank manager had told us in 2019 that we could both retire "right now and you'll be fine." But she was just speaking about objective reality. Who uses *that* as a guide to the rest of their lives?! Far easier to not look at the numbers and stew.

By April I was in a different world. The threat Covid presented may have been vague and far off, but that made no difference to my psyche. With every passing day, I grew more anxious, less able to sleep and concentrate. I also realized that I'd go stir-crazy and drive Jean crazy, as well, if I had nothing to do. Losing 90 percent of my income is one thing; losing 90 percent of what I do all day was even worse.

So I decided that I would write a blog. I'd tried to do this years before. But after a few weeks, it petered out in the face of "real" writing, plus our hyperactive social and travel lives. Now was different. I had all day to write, and since we never saw anyone or went anywhere, all night, too. If not now, when?

I called the blog *The Plague-Ground*, and it was going to be about our lives in the pandemic. I had no idea how often I'd write it, or even what I'd say. I wasn't in the front lines. I was in hiding. Besides, every writer on earth had something to say about this never-in-the-history-of-the-world event. So I decided to write about the little things and my reaction to them. Here's what I wrote in my first blog about the day before we left the city:

> My 39-year-old step-daughter dropped off some toilet paper at our condo this morning. While we don't need toilet paper, I was touched by her gesture. In return, I gave her one of our three tubes of Clorox Disinfecting Wipes.
>
> Before last week, that interaction would have been unnecessary, unthinkable, preposterous. Today, it's a tale of love in the time of coronavirus.
>
> Like billions of families for thousands of years, we exchange things our kids don't really need because we can and we care and we're family. These gifts don't just have great sentimental value. Toilet paper and disinfecting wipes are now, in our pre-plague economy, rare and precious.
>
> We then talked for 15 minutes with her standing awkwardly in the entranceway to our condo and me sitting at the dining room table. I didn't offer her coffee. She didn't move closer.

I also didn't know who would ever read *The Plague-Ground*. But since I was no longer hosting speaker events or group trips,

I had little to lose by sending it to my entire five-thousand-name mailing list. Yes, that's a lot of people. Do I really know all of them? Not all, no. Some have signed on as one-time guests at one of our lunches.

But mostly I do know them. Hundreds have been getting emails and notes from me for thirty years. I love people. Some say I collect them. Well, I certainly love connecting them. And by April of 2020, who knew where keeping in touch with all of them could lead? Having lost nearly all my business, I had little to lose by reminding my friends I had something to say.

Like so many ideas born in the pandemic, my motives for writing *The Plague-Ground* had little to do with the ultimate result. For me, it was all about forcing myself to sit down and write seven hundred publishable words up to five days a week. But even more, it was about having a voice, being seen, and staying in the game. And my fundamental fear of losing all that drove me to keep writing.

But that wasn't my only fear, or my worst.

One night in April, Jean and I were talking about the news that doctors in Toronto may have to decide which very ill Covid patients get put on ventilators, and which don't. No ventilator meant a slow, agonizing, and certain death.

I said offhand to Jean that because she's a doctor and in far better shape than most seventy-seven-year-olds, I was certain they'd put her on a ventilator.

To this Jean replied, "It doesn't matter, because I'd refuse the ventilator, anyway."

"What?"

And thus began the most frightening fight of our lives.

Jean began. "If there's a shortage of ventilators, they should give mine to someone younger. I don't need to be at the front of the line."

"But you'd die."

"I could. But, dear, we have a system and it doesn't work if someone like me can change the rules. Besides, I don't want to die all alone in a hospital."

"But, darling, you're talking about your life here. You'd give it up to be fair to the system?"

"Yes, I would."

I was stunned. It's one thing to pay lip service to equal access. But when it's your life on the line, then all rules go out the window. That's what I'd been brought up to believe. Apparently, Jean hadn't.

"Honey, when my time comes, it comes. I've seen plenty of people die. I *help* people die. Dying on a ventilator is not how I want to die."

I was panicked. "So you're saying that if you get Covid and you need to go to the ER, it's game over for you?"

"If I get sicker, yes."

"Well, I'm not going to let you die. I have power of attorney for your health. I'll tell them to put you on a ventilator."

"No, you won't."

And there we stood, glaring at each other. Me terrified that my wife somehow wanted to wish her own death. Jean determined to play by the rules, even at the cost of her life.

Now, to be clear, this conversation took place over three nights. Back and forth we went.

Knowing when this happened gives you a better sense of just how terrified I was. It was mid-April. Cases were starting to rise. Hundreds, no, thousands of Italians were dying. New Yorkers were being infected in droves. No one had enough ventilators. No one knew how the virus spread. But we all knew it attacked old people fiercely.

The distant unknown threat was far more frightening than any clear and present danger. Which also accounted for a strange lethargy that overcame me back then. I would sleep for hours and wake up exhausted. Weekdays flowed into weekends. I consumed days of Netflix. It was little comfort to know the entire world was feeling pretty much like this, too.

But I did have one very clear task: to keep my wife from getting sick. Because if she got sick, even a little, it was clear to me, she would die. I didn't know what angered me more: the prospect of her dying or her determination to let fate have its way. For a control freak like me, to be presented with this reality — by the woman I love so much — took my fear into strange, new, and frightening territory. It's one thing to not be able to help someone you love. It's a different dimension when they can help themselves — and refuse. At least that's how I framed it in a desperate attempt to wrest some tiny bit of control from the logic of Jean's argument.

Forget that we weren't living in exactly a coronavirus hot spot, or that we'd moved our lives up north precisely for this reason. Rational thought had nothing to do with what drove me that month. When the handyman who fixes things at our cottage came around one day, unmasked and not really into social distancing, I nearly pushed him out the door in panic.

A week after our first argument, I heard Jean talking on the phone with her doctor and medical partner, Mary Rubino, who's been a great friend of ours for thirty years. The subject was Jean's "Advance Directive for Care." She'd designated me as the person to determine if the doctors should ever have to pull the plug, and her sister, Joyce, was the backup.

But now she seemed to be asking Mary if she would put her name on this document; if she would take my place; if she would do what I refused to.

When Jean hung up, I asked her what she was talking with Mary about.

"I want her to have my power of attorney for health."

"Don't I have that?"

"You do. But you've made it clear that you won't carry out my wishes, so I've asked my doctor, who's said she will."

My betrayal was total. How could she? How dare she? She'd gone behind my back, dismissed me like an errant schoolboy.

"Were you even going to tell me?!" I yelled at her.

"Of course I was. But at least give me a minute after I hang up the phone with Mary, will you?"

I'd never felt more helpless in my life. All my fears of rejection and uselessness came to a head at this precise moment. Not to mention, how could I not save Jean's life when she had saved mine?

Of course, this was just my view. Jean's defiance and belief in equal health care for all would end up killing her — and by extension, me.

A great friend reminded me that this encounter wasn't actually about me. It was about Jean. And if Jean felt this way, then I'd just better get used to it.

She also reminded me that Jean knew a lot more about end-of-life care than I ever would. If anyone had a right to feel threatened, it was Jean, who no longer had confidence that her husband would carry out her wishes. So she put them in the hands of someone who would.

Meanwhile, living for six months in your country cottage during a pandemic can change other home truths, as well. One of these was, where do we call "home"? We are city folk through and through. Many weekends we'd drive up to stay at our cottage. These had grown to three-day weekends, from Friday afternoon to Monday morning.

But the pandemic showed us that we don't have to physically be somewhere in order to do our work. It only took me a few weeks to move the RamsayTalks online and to start teaching online, as well. As the host and teacher, I could be literally anywhere, provided I had strong Wi-Fi. RamsayTravels stayed dormant, as the world came to realize that going anywhere in the fall of 2020 was risky and that no big travel would happen until later in 2021.

This didn't keep our own travel bug under the rug. Though Jean and I couldn't go to our favourite fishing lodge in northern B.C. last summer, we did turn our love for sea kayaking into three separate week-long expeditions — one up Georgian Bay, one on Lake Superior, and one around Manitoulin Island. As a friend said, we were practising extreme social distancing.

All these trips reminded me of when we're at our best with each other: camping on a rock on Georgian Bay, with the wind howling through our thin tent, the thunder clapping, and lightning flashing. Ah, to feel so alive all the time.

By August, I was back in business. It turned out that sending five thousand people a brief blog five days a week will persuade some of them that you know how to write, and if you offer them a course in better business writing, they'll sign up for it. And as my big financial clients moved their entire operations online, I followed gratefully in their wake.

Jean was going through even bigger changes. She'd planned to run the Boston Marathon in April 2020. They expected their eight-time age-group winner from Toronto. But the lockdown in March postponed the April race to September, and by June, the world's most storied marathon was moved to April 2021.

It wasn't this that brought Jean to stop training for Boston and to retire from marathoning, though that was pretty discouraging. It was her sense that driving herself mercilessly up and down the country roads every month of the year was now getting pretty pointless.

She was slowing down, tiring more easily, able to run less far. When I suggested that it could possibly have something to do with age, she scoffed, as she'd always done. But I think the pain of running ten to twenty miles a day when you're seventy-seven years old can easily outrun the rewards. She'd never say so, but this was her first acknowledgement that she can't just keep running forever.

She didn't stop running; she just stopped training. She also got a bike and, of course, those kayak expeditions weren't just lunch and learns. But so much of her identity, or at least how the world identified her, was wrought up in marathoning that it was actually good to see her wind it up herself and not have to be dragged off some course or get injured.

Jean's work changed even more profoundly.

She said that she'd retire from family practice at the end of 2019 and as the months ticked to that goal, far from pushing it further away, which she'd done for many years, she raced toward it. By June, she couldn't wait to quit. Again, this was a surprise. I think treating her patients through her computer took away some of the incredible intimacy she'd enjoyed in helping them face to face. This was especially true with her MAiD patients, who were requesting Medical Assistance in Dying. Before Covid, she would assess them in person, but during Covid, that truly life-or-death encounter had to take place online. Once a month, Jean would drive back down to Toronto to help a patient die. In the spring, it was pretty gruesome. Only one family member, Jean, a nurse, and the patient. Almost as lonely as dying on a ventilator. By August, with some distancing restrictions lifted, not only could family members gather, but some patients who had obtained permission for MAiD suddenly changed their minds. It was summer. They could go outside. It was gorgeous, and they could be with their families once more. Which tells you what we live for in the end.

That, too, changed with us. Jean's kids and our two grandkids quickly saw that our cottage could be their "sanctuary home," at least during the summer, and up they all came.

It was glorious: getting to know our six-year-old granddaughter and four-year-old grandson changed them, changed us, and changed the entire family dynamic. Using a combination of couch-es, bunkies, and boltholes, everyone in the family could be with us at the same time. For a person like me and a couple like us, this was amazing. A miracle. Teaching my grandson how to light a fire was a huge thrill, and "sploring" in the woods with him filled me with memories good and bad of my own childhood. So this was how functional families worked!

All to say Jean and I agreed that our cottage would become our principal residence, in fact, if not in name, and that our condo at Pape and Danforth would be our *pied-à-terre* in the city.

This small name change in our conversation reflected a much bigger change in our minds.

Now, we'd spend four to five days a week up north, and two to three in the city. Not for all months. Georgian Bay can be pretty bleak in January and February. But during Covid we'd spent more time in the same place together than we ever did before. This con-stant bumping into each other took some getting used to. But we each found our space and made it work.

This change sparked another. Rather than heading south in the winter for a couple of weeks, why not do that for a couple of months, instead? The destination would have to have great Wi-Fi and "be safe." But what was out of the question in 2020 might now actually happen in late 2021. Besides, couldn't I be a digital nomad and wasn't Jean retiring, anyway?

Well, yes and no. She'd give up family practice. But never her assisted-death work. From the moment she began doing MAiD in 2016, helping people die well became the driving force in why she practised medicine. Part of it was novelty. She'd done family medi-cine for forty-six years and MAiD for four. But a bigger part is that as she approached the years of her own death, she appreciated being able to help the sickest, frailest people whose circumstances are of-ten the most tragic.

Besides, as she said, "With MAiD, you can only get sued for malpractice if the patient doesn't die."

There is that, yes.

She's writing a book about MAiD, as well, a book that, because of Covid, will come out in the spring of 2022. She's co-authoring it with *Globe and Mail* journalist Johanna Schneller, and it's the story of how a small group of doctors back in 2016 trained up for a new medical specialty made possible by a Supreme Court decision, a specialty in which no one knew anything, and that many people viewed as akin to murder.

The Last Doctor is that story, combined with stories of the patients — and their families — who chose this route to end their lives.

EPILOGUE   Death by Doctor

It's hard to be married to a doctor whose profession is putting people to death, and to have some near-death experiences myself, and *not* fantasize about my wife ending my own life.

The odds of this happening are zero, of course, because doctors aren't allowed to treat their spouses, let alone to kill them. But that's just real life. Fantasies are much more powerful, at least for me.

Mine goes like this: As Jean predicted, I will likely stroke out, which means that the mini-stroke I had in 2019 will return with a vengeance. Or my heart's rhythm will move from being occasionally out of synch to being wildly so, beating faster and faster until it finally stops, exhausted. Or my bladder cancer will metastasize.

With a history like this, you can see why I don't even bother applying for insurance.

What I don't want to be when I die is alone. That would frighten me to … well, any prospect of comfort at the end would be overwhelmed by the sheer terror of facing my end on my own. I've never been a fan of living alone; dying alone would be much worse. I'm also afraid of dying in great pain. Jean once said that I don't have a low pain threshold; I have a low threshold around my fear of pain. The prospect of gasping to death or groaning in cancerous agony is not one I have the courage to face.

So I'm a prime candidate for medically assisted death. And if I don't really qualify, I count on my wife to help me, anyway. At least in my dreams. There's a scene in *Still Alice*, the film adaptation of Lisa Genova's novel, where Julianne Moore plays a professor who gets early-onset Alzheimer's. Knowing her condition will get worse, she stashes away some pills to do away with herself when she's more demented. But when that day comes and she searches frantically for her pills, she can't find them because, of course, she can't remember where she hid them. I watched that scene in horror.

It wasn't the loss of connection or capability that frightened me so much; it was the loss of control. Which I guess has been the defining arc through my life and this memoir of it.

I said to Jean after the movie that if I was diagnosed with early-onset Alzheimer's, I would stash those sedatives in a thousand different places so that, no matter how anxious and forgetful I grew, I would quickly find enough to end my days just by closing my eyes.

Jean looked askance, as she always does whenever my sense of entitlement gets the better of me. And *possibly* she's right. After all, this is the ultimate in drug-seeking behaviour, something that's dogged me too many of my days.

When I look back on Jean's and my thirty years together, I'm reminded of what Søren Kierkegaard said: "Life can only be understood backwards; but it must be lived forwards."

We are not the kind of people who dwell much on the past, though my attachment to its blows and joys has held me in that distant land too long. We just keep moving at what the world sees as a feverish pace. Maybe if we talked about the past, that hold would loosen and make it easier to stay calm and carry on to the time in our lives when things will really start to break down, when we will grow tired and irrelevant.

Then again, it's not that our lives are unexamined. I think anyone who makes it into their seventies has a pretty good sense of who they are and aren't, and what they can change and can't. Age may not soften you, but it does accommodate your eccentricities more kindly.

One thing we will never do is forget how we each rescued the other when we were both at the bottom of our lives. How Jean changed me and I changed Jean. How we knew what to leave alone, to carve out our own space within the relationship. Our two dominating personalities knew that if one of us tried to swallow the other, that gulp would be our last.

It's been a wild ride and we'll only gear down when the curves ahead order us to.

ACKNOWLEDGEMENTS

This book grew out of an article I wrote for *Maclean's* in 2012 about my near-death experience following open-heart surgery.

By "grew" I don't mean "expanded." I mean stalled and disbanded. It took two people to get me back on track. The first was Michael Levine, who's had my back for over forty years, both as friend and literary agent. With one sentence, "Write a love story, not a death story," he set this book back in motion. The second was Patrick Crean, one of Canada's most storied book editors, who over our biannual sushi lunches would implore me, "Make it a book, Bob, because it is one."

This is a recovery memoir in the widest sense of that term: recovery from addiction, from franticness, from fear — and into love. If anyone should wave the flag of gratitude, it's me. So to my friends Ian Yolles and Ron Estey; to the late Arthur Gelgoot and Charles Fremes, all of whom intervened on me; to the professionals at Talbott Recovery Center in Atlanta, whose tough love broke me down in order to build me up; to Dr. Carolyn Bennett, who introduced me to the woman who would become my wife; to my business manager of forty years, Joan Fischer, who, when I was losing my mind, made sure I didn't lose my shirt, as well; and to the many, *many* friends whose concern and love held me together, in sickness and in health, I want to say that I'm really only here, for better or for worse, because of you. Thank you.

I also want to single out Jean's now-very-adult children: Lara, Jean Paul, and Ryan. When I walked into your lives thirty years ago, my sense was that you all had a single thought: "Mom, have you lost your mind?," which any teenage kid would think. But here we all are, operating as a frequently functioning family. So thank you for your patience, tolerance, and, when it was needed, distance.

As for this book, the first serious reader was my colleague Julia McDowell, who has gone on to her own career in publishing. She never stopped prodding: "But Bob, how did that make you *feel*?!"

At my publisher, I'd like to thank Kathryn Lane, Elena Radic, and Russell Smith, for keeping me both on time and in my own lane. A special thanks also to Paul Haslip of HM&E Design Communications for creating a cover that captures both the fire and the ice of what's inside.

Finally, first and foremost, I want to thank my wife, Jean, whose love is the driving force in my life and this book. When I called my friend Costa Pilavachi to tell him in 2016 how Jean had sensed, diagnosed, then got us back home from Asia just in time to halt a fatal condition, he asked with an air of resignation, "*How* many times has that woman saved your life?"

Well, yes, there is that. But lifesaver doesn't really describe the life Jean and I have created for each other. So I thank her for saving one life and building two together.

ABOUT THE AUTHOR

Bob Ramsay is the president of the Toronto communications firm Ramsay Inc. and the founder of the speaker's series RamsayTalks.

Bob was born in Edmonton and graduated with a B.A. in English from Princeton. He writes frequent opinion pieces for the mainline media, and during the pandemic wrote the popular blog *The Plague-Ground*.

For many years, he was the fundraising chair on the board of the Toronto International Film Festival (TIFF) and an executive board member of the Canadian Film Centre. He's also served on the boards of the St. Lawrence Centre, the Women's College Hospital Foundation, and the International Festival of Authors, which he also chaired.

Bob was awarded the Queen Elizabeth II Diamond Jubile Medal in 2015 and the Bernier Medal from the Royal Canadi Geographical Society in 2017. He is also a member of the Explo Club in New York.

ABOUT THE AUTHOR

Bob Ramsay is the president of the Toronto communications firm Ramsay Inc. and the founder of the speaker's series RamsayTalks.

Bob was born in Edmonton and graduated with a B.A. in English from Princeton. He writes frequent opinion pieces for the mainline media, and during the pandemic wrote the popular blog *The Plague-Ground*.

For many years, he was the fundraising chair on the board of the Toronto International Film Festival (TIFF) and an executive board member of the Canadian Film Centre. He's also served on the boards of the St. Lawrence Centre, the Women's College Hospital Foundation, and the International Festival of Authors, which he also chaired.

Bob was awarded the Queen Elizabeth II Diamond Jubilee Medal in 2015 and the Bernier Medal from the Royal Canadian Geographical Society in 2017. He is also a member of the Explorers Club in New York.